SCURVY DOGS, GREEN WATER AND GUNSMOKE

FIFTY YEARS IN U.S. NAVY DESTROYERS

SCURVY DOGS, GREEN WATER AND GUNSMOKE

FIFTY YEARS IN U.S. NAVY DESTROYERS

Edited by Bob Cohen and Terry Miller

Oak Tree Press   Taylorville, IL

Oak Tree Press books may be purchased for educational, business or sales promotional purposes. Contact Publisher for quantity discounts.

First Edition, March 2008

Cover design by MickA Design.com

Cover photo courtesy of Battleship Cove, Fall River, Massachusetts.

First Navy Jack image courtesy of *www.NavyJack.info*.

Library of Congress Cataloging-in-Publication Data

Scurvy dogs, green water and gunsmoke : fifty years in U.S. Navy destroy-ers / edited by Robert Cohen and Terry Miller. -- 1st ed.
    p. cm.
  ISBN 978-1-892343-06-2 (vol 1 : alk. paper) -- ISBN 978-1-892343-07-9 (vol 2 : alk. paper)
1. Destroyers (Warships)--United States--Anecdotes. 2. Destroyers (Warships)--United States--History--20th century. 3. United States. Navy--Anecdotes. 4. Sailors--United States--Biography. I. Cohen, Robert B., 1959- II. Miller, Terry L., 1946-
  V825.3.S36 2008
  359.3'254092273--dc22

                                        2007052300

All authors' royalties from the sale of this book are being donated to the Navy-Marine Corps Relief Society, in memory of Lance Corporal Shane Lee Goldman, 3rd Platoon - Charlie Company, 1st Battalion, 5th Marine Regiment, 1st Marine Division, KIA 05 April 2004, ar-Ramadi, Iraq.

Preface

From: \<Verner Newman\>
To: \<Secret Scurvy Dog Society\>
Subject: YOUNGBLOOD
Sent: March 20, 2002

March 20, 1950, Verner L. Newman III entered the hallowed halls of USNS San Diego, Ca, to start paying his dues to all who got in his way on his march to admiralty. That was until he discovered on his first trip down 4th St. that they had ice cold Budweiser, Anzio, & Gallo wine. To come over 1500 miles from the land of wheat, potatoes, & virgins to the sandy shores by the big blue Pacific to become corrupted by early to rise early to bed, marching to meals, classes, church, to take a shit, get a hair cut, wash clothes, jack off in a sock, saluting CPO because we didn't know any better, besides they all looked alike, blonde & blue, going to class to learn how to don't shoot until you see the whites of their eyes, which seemed sort of dumb especially all of the enemy had whites around their eyes unless it was full red from studying all night because you didn't want to fail & get set back. Eating baked beans on Saturday morning & march from India street to Balboa park with all the little kids lining the streets laughing at your, what they thought to be the biggest feet in the world, not knowing that all the shoes were 4 sizes too large. Giving blood on Saturday because the CPO said they would kick your ass if you didn't, then wouldn't take my blood because I had a temp, but the drunks gave & received 72 hour passes, but I had to go back to the barracks & the socks, (washing clothes, what did you think?), graduating with honors, made the color guard until it was found out I was making history, sent to mess cooking, supposed to be going to disbursing school, missed my ship, flew to Treasure Island, stood in a 300 man shot line from 0800 until 1200 waving my shot card & big ass shoes, very white T shirt under my chin, neckerchief squared at the vee, brand new clothes, dumb boot, looking good, still standing until I finally got to the head only to be told I didn't need any shots, I wasn't nothing but a dumb boot who had missed his ship again, go to Alameda & fly to Diego just in time to receive the foul weather passages as my cleaning station as the ship got under way for Pearl, having the Captain welcoming me aboard & chewing my ass out because of some dirt no one could see anyway, besides I didn't put it there, went topside watching the old hands waving & crying, started singing "Red Sails in the Sunset," they all got pissed at me & wanted to kick my ass, hell I was happy I was going over seas, no age limit, whores, paid twice a week, fuck them. Four years, 3 ships 2 combat tours (21 months over seas) still seaman 1st, took ROTC passed, got to prep school, sent back to the ship, didn't have enough teeth, Navy pulled 2, my career & dreams of becoming an admiral got very, very dim, damn dark. So here I am, March 20, 2002, sitting here in front of my computer talking to a bunch of old, but younger ex gobs, sea gull green shit colored jarheads a few officers who couldn't get a job anywhere else, some ex police officers who were much better off in the fleet but won't admit it. Happy birthday old Salt, have many nonalcoholic beers & do what you use to tell grand ma you were doing when she would say, "boy, you better quit blowing snot in your socks."

Contributors

Len Barrett is a retired Master Chief Operations Specialist. During his thirty-year career (from 1961 to 1991) he served on several destroyers and other class ships in both an active and reserve status. Len's story appears in Volume 1.

Dave Carlson served on active duty from 1973 to 1979 as a Fire Control Technician (guns). He served aboard two destroyers, one cruiser and one tender. He now lives in White Bear Lake, Minnesota and works as a Quality Assurance Engineer. Dave's stories appear on pages 43 and 141.

Bob Cohen was the first reserve midshipman in the Navy to qualify as an offshore yacht skipper in 1980. He later served as an engineer on the *USS Whipple (FF-1062)* and the *USS Henry B. Wilson (DDG-7)*. He left the Navy in 1984 and is now a retired NYPD captain. Bob's stories appear on pages 24, 37, 75, 83, and 132.

Ken Dandurand of Sioux City, Iowa, was a Hull Technician who came into and went out of the Navy on destroyers. In between, from 1961 to 1982, he served on many other ships. He was the first sailor in the Navy to qualify for the Enlisted Surface Warfare Specialist Program. He currently is retired in Colorado. Ken's stories appear on pages 34, 71, 87, and 91.

Jack Dineen was an Operations Specialist aboard the *USS King (DDG-41)* from 1978 to 1981 and is a past Vice President of the USS King Association. He is also an associate member of the Fraternal Order of UDT/SEALS. Retired from the NYPD, he resides in New York City with his wife and daughter and presently works as a Maritime Security Specialist for Secure Ocean Service LLC of Virginia Beach, Virginia. Jack's story appears on page 166.

Arnold Hofmann, a retired Supply Corps Commander, served aboard *USS McKean (DD-784)* from 1969 to 1971. He is married and lives in Washington State, where he is a duly-licensed Master Mariner. Arnie's stories appear on page 47 and 133.

Dave Hood was an ASROC Gunner's Mate on the *USS McKean (DD-784)*. He spent a year in the Army National Guard crewing Hueys and Cobras and then spent four years with a Navy Special Warfare Unit. He spends his free time in undisclosed Latin American countries. When north of the Rio Grande he lives in Washington State with his wife Elaine. Dave's stories appear on pages 45, 55, 81, 109, and 122.

Jim Kelly, born in Margaretville, NY, served in *USS William R. Rush (DD-714)* as a Gunner's Mate (guns) from 1970 to 1973. Past President, USS Wm. R. Rush Association, he is currently the Historian for the association. He is married with two daughters, living in North Carolina. Jim's story appears on page 176.

Richard H. King served as a junior officer aboard the *USS Chevalier (DD-805)* from 1965 to 1968, most significantly as the Main Propulsion Assistant. After that tour he joined the ready reserves while attending law school and is now a retired lawyer, developer and Naval Reserve Commander living in Nashville, Tennessee. Dick's stories appear on pages 20, 27, 50, 63, 138, and 157.

G. Ben Miller III served on the *USS Henry B. Wilson (DDG-7)* from 1978 to 1982 as a Machinist's Mate. Self-employed from 1983 to 2004, he is now working for the El Dorado County Sheriff's Department in Placerville, California. Ben's stories appear in Volume 1.

Terry Miller served as a Sonar Technician aboard *USS George K. MacKenzie (DD-836)* from 1968 to 1970. He is currently Executive Director, Tin Can Sailors, Inc., President of the USS George K. MacKenzie Association, and the Associate Member Representative on the Board of Historic Naval Ships Association. He is married with two grown daughters and lives in Texas with his wife, Camella. Terry's stories appear on pages 68, 78, 85, 130, and 150.

 **Verner Newman III** joined the reserves in 1947 and three years later enlisted in the regular Navy, serving aboard the *USS McKean (DD-784)*, *Everett (PF-8)* and *Chevalier (DD-805)* during the Korean War. He went on to a career as a captain in the Lawrence Police Department, and then to yet another career as a manager in Kansas state government. He is now a full-time senior citizen, babysitter and sports advocate. Verner's story is the preface to this Volume.

 **Larry Pallozola** served as a Fire Control Technician (guns) on the *USS McKean (DD-784)*, and also briefly onboard the *USS Long Beach (CGN-9)* as well as in the reserves. He currently lives on the beach in Seattle, happily married, and is looking forward to retirement. Larry's story is on page 179.

 **Carl Sims** served aboard the *USS Basilone (DD-824)* from 1966 through 1970 as a Fire Control Technician (guns). Taking advantage of the GI bill after service, Carl earned a Masters degree in chemistry from Northern Arizona University and currently is a senior scientist for the IDEX corporation. Married with two grown children, Carl and his wife Lynn reside in Saint Paul, Minnesota. Carl's story appears on page 38.

 **Robin Smith** was a Quartermaster aboard the *USS Spruance (DD-963)* from 1974 to 1978. Married with three kids, he is currently a research physicist for the Naval Research Laboratory, and lives in Virginia. Robin's stories appear on pages 115, 126, 136, 144, 151, and 172.

Mike Snyder served twenty-four years active duty aboard numerous ships including three destroyers. Retiring as a Lieutenant Commander in 1983, Mike worked in FFG-7 combat systems support for twenty more years and earned an MS in Technology Management from the University of Maryland. He and his wife Jean retired again to San Rafael, California in 2005 to live near their children. Mike's stories appear on pages 76, 80, 97, 103, 112, and 148.

Robert teGroen served on the *USS Ernest G. Small (DDR-838)* as a Machinist's Mate during the Korean War and later served thirty years as a drilling reservist on a variety of tin cans and other ships. He is a retired sergeant from the Los Angeles Police Department and lives in northern California. Robert's stories appear on pages 32, 95, 100, and 164.

Gary White is a former Sonar Technician who served aboard *USS Mahan (DLG-11)* and *USS George K. MacKenzie (DD-836)* from 1968 to 1970. He is Secretary-Treasurer of the USS Mahan Association and works as a business credit professional. He and his wife, Kay, live in Texas. Gary's stories appear on pages 17, 40, and 61.

Thanks to Keith Bettinger, Jack Casey, Peter Papadakos, Chris Whitten and the late Tom Peltin.

In Harm's Way

ALLEN M. SUMNER CLASS

Length: 376' Displacement: 2200 tons 70 built, in service 1944-1975

RD3 Len Barrett
OI Division, USS Maddox (DD-731) 1964

RD2 Len Barrett
OI Division, USS Maddox (DD-731) 1970*

MMC Robert teGroen
M Division, USS Maddox (DD-731) 1969-73*

(* Selected Reserves)

EPITAPH FOR A DRAGON

THE SINKING OF USS MCKEAN

BY GARY WHITE

Like many of her sister ships, the *USS McKean*, originally *DD-90*, a four-stack destroyer of the *Wickes*-class, was laid down at the height of the "war to end all wars" in 1918. By the time she reached commission on 25 February 1919, peace was beginning to settle over Europe and her mission became one of routine tours off the Atlantic Coast with a single cruise to European waters in mid-1919. She was decommissioned in 1922 and placed in the reserve fleet at the Philadelphia Navy Yard, where she rested for the next eighteen years.

By mid-1940, with Hitler rolling across Europe and the potential threat of war with Japan looming larger each day, the Navy began recommissioning and converting four-stackers for duty as small, fast assault ships, capable of transporting a moderate number of troops. The *McKean*, one of the first six, was reclassified *APD-5* on 2 August 1940 and recommissioned on 11 December of that same year. With a draught of only 8½ feet and a top speed of 35 knots (26 after modification to remove the forward fire room for extra troop carrying capacity) these reconfigured four-stackers made up in speed and maneuverability what they lacked in armaments.

The *McKean* arrived in the South Pacific in late July 1942, ready to take an active role as a member of Transport Division 12. The ships with their camouflage paint schemes, a mottled green and gray in large diagonal stripes, were promptly dubbed *Green Dragons* by the Marine raiders they transported. She landed her first troops at Tulagi on 7 August 1942 and for the next several months made escort and supply runs from bases at New Caledonia and the New Hebrides to troop positions in the southern Solomon Islands. She departed the Pacific theater in late January 1943 for an overhaul, returning in mid-June of that same year to resume her escort and patrol operations. From July to November, she patrolled the waters around Guadalcanal and up "the Slot" as well as landing troops on New Georgia and Rendova. In late October, she landed troops at Mono Island and on 6 November landed Marines near Cape Tokorina, Empress Augusta Bay, and Bougainville. On 11 November, she made a second run with Marine raiders to Bougainville and returned to Guadalcanal to pick up more "Fifth Echelon" troops bound for Cape Tokorina.

After embarking a 185-man contingent of the 21st Regiment, 3rd Marine Division, the *McKean*, along with the other APDs of Transport Divisions 12 and 22, the *USS Stringham (APD-6)*, the *USS Talbot (APD-7)*, the *USS Waters (APD-8)*, the *USS Dent (APD-9)*, the *USS Kilty (APD-15)*, the *USS Ward (APD-16)*, and the *USS Crosby (APD-17)*, sailed from Guadalcanal late on 15 November 1943 for a dawn rendezvous south of Simbo Island with the remaining units of Task Group 31.6. It would be the *McKean's* 23rd and final mission.

The rendezvous, routine and uneventful, linked the six destroyers of DesRon 22, the *USS Renshaw (DD-499)* with Commander Task Group 31.6 aboard, the *USS Saufley (DD-465)*, the *USS Waller (DD-466)*, the *USS Pringle (DD-477)*, the *USS Conway (DD-507)*, and the *USS Sigourney (DD-643)*, as well as LSTs 70, 207, 339, 341, 353, 354, 395 and 488 of LST Flotilla Five with the APDs. Shortly after departing the rendezvous point, the ocean-going fleet tug *Pawnee (AT-74)* joined the Task Group to become its last member.

John Ryan, a Navy corpsman assigned to the 21st Regiment remembers: "When we left the 'Canal' we were told that there was a good possibility we would be attacked by Japanese aircraft and to go below decks if an air raid should occur. Most of us ignored the advice and decided to stay on deck to watch the fireworks."

The convoy, with five of the six destroyers forming an anti-aircraft, anti-submarine outer ring, and the eight APDs as an inner defense ring enjoyed a quiet passage. The eight LSTs, in Charlie One formation (a box configuration with Pawnee in the box's middle) and the *Renshaw* ahead of the starboard lead LST comprised the convoy's center. The *McKean*, steaming at 13 knots, was zigzagging 30 to 50 degrees either side of the base course at the rear of the formation acting as anti-submarine patrol.

At 3:00 a.m., 17 November, as the convoy approached Empress Augusta Bay, radar detected several bogies. Ten minutes later one of the bogies, now identified as a "Val"-type Japanese torpedo plane, made an attack on the *Waller* but was hit by gunfire and downed before releasing its torpedo. Thirty minutes later, another of the aircraft began what appeared to be an attack on the *Talbot*, to starboard of the *McKean*. Suddenly, the plane turned sharply to the right, directly at the *McKean*. The *McKean's* captain, LCDR Ralph Ramey, ordered the helm full left to provide a smaller target for the plane. The *McKean* opened fire with her starboard 20mm *pom-poms*, choosing not to use her 3" main battery for fear of hitting the *Talbot*.

Gene LaMere, an electrician aboard the *McKean*, whose battle station was manning a search light on the mast, recalls: "It was dark but I had a good view from the mast. I managed to see the plane as he dropped his torpedo. I saw the torpedo wake go under the starboard quarter near the stern. It took a little time for the fish to explode and I was starting to think it had run too deep and missed us, but at that time, it went off. It blew my search light off of the mast and stunned me."

At 3:50 a.m., the torpedo struck home, immediately exploding the after magazines and depth charge stowage. This, in turn, ruptured the diesel fuel tanks, throwing burning oil throughout the after part of the ship. Aft of the #1 stack, the ship was a mass of flames; of the crew stationed aft, only three survived the blast and heat, the three having been blown overboard by the explosion. Debris falling across the siren cord caused the siren to sound continuously, giving the event an added touch of the surreal.

During the attack the starboard 20mm mount continued to fire at the plane. They realized success too late; the "Val" crashed just ahead of the ship moments after the torpedo exploded.

John Wrocklage, assigned as a shell loader on the number two 5-inch mount aboard the *Conway* says of the moment: "We heard a tremendous explosion and opened the gun hatch, only to see that a ship had been badly hit, was all aflame and on the verge of sinking."

As the *McKean*, now without power, began to slow down, some members of the troop contingent began abandoning ship. Nearly all who did so were dragged into the burning oil and perished. At 4:10 a.m., 20 minutes after being hit, Abandon Ship was ordered and all remaining crew and Marines went over the side. Five minutes later, both the forward diesel tank and magazine exploded almost simultaneously, disintegrating the forward part of the ship. By 4:18 a.m., it was all over for the *McKean*. She settled stern first, coming to rest peacefully in 75 fathoms of water about 22 miles off Bougainville. As she neared the ocean floor, two of her depth charges exploded; a final salute for a worthy ship. Of the six original APD in Transport Division 12, only the *Manley* and the *Stringham* remained. The APDs had proved their worth, however. These ships, despite their shortcomings, had shown their unique ability to implement their part of the strategic plan for pursuing the war in the Pacific.

The survivors, now in the water, continued to tend to those more seriously injured or too tired to swim. Rescue boats from the *Waller*, the *Talbot* and the *Sigourney*, ordered by ComTaskGrp to stand off and pick up survivors, reported many instances of being told by those in the water to pick up the injured first. The rescue, carried off without a mishap, was even more amazing given the fact that all three ships were under constant air attack as they maneuvered around picking up survivors. Waiting to be rescued, John Ryan says, "While floating around out there, one Marine said, 'Hey Doc, would you like a cigarette?' I said, 'Who the hell are you trying to kid?' The Marine replied, 'No, I got a pack of waterproof cigarettes,' and we sat out there and smoked while floating around watching the destroyers trying to shoot down the Jap planes." Enemy aircraft continued to attack the remainder of the convoy until after sunrise when fighters from Air Sols arrived to provide cover for the landing.

The final tally showed that of the 12 officers and 141 enlisted men comprising the *McKean's* crew, 64 lost their lives as a result of the sinking. Among the 185 Marines embarked, 52 died. But what has remained alive among the survivors for the half century since the loss of the *McKean* is a sense of mutual respect. Says Bill Hoysradt, a signalman aboard the *McKean*, "I always have had a great respect for the Marines as I felt lucky that all we had to do was get them there." And Jerry White, Sergeant, Headquarters Co., 3rd Battalion, 21st Regiment once said, "The Navy, as always, did a remarkable job that night. It was the only reason I survived." That quote was spoken to me years ago by Sgt. White. You see, he survived to become my father.

KOOL FILTER KINGS AND BLEU CHEESE

BY DICK KING

I started smoking in high school, where I was furnished with Kool Filter Kings by a friend who stole them from his stepfather. I continued smoking Kools in college and got to the point that I didn't like any other brand. Kools are strong with lots of menthol. No other brand is quite like them.

After college and a belated midshipman cruise aboard a minesweeper, I arrived on board the *USS Chevalier (DD-805)* in the late summer of 1965 with the rank of ensign. For some purposes, such as saluting, an ensign is higher than a chief petty officer, higher even than a chief warrant officer, but lower than a lieutenant (junior grade). However, for practical purposes, new ensigns fall somewhere in between third class and second class petty officers.

Shortly after my arrival, the *Chevalier* went to the yards at Hunter's Point, San Francisco, and the ship was declared uninhabitable. I ended up sharing a large apartment in San Francisco with four other officers, including the Supply Officer, LTJG Dave Hartman. After returning to San Diego, I then shared a beach house with Hartman again, plus Ensign Jim Culotta, the DASH Officer. As we readied for the WestPac deployment in early 1966, I impressed upon my twice-roommate and friend, Dave Hartman, to make sure the ship's store didn't run out of Kool Filter Kings halfway around the world. I reminded him again and again, and he assured me that he would, then that he had, taken aboard a huge supply.

Sometime around the middle of our deployment, while we were assigned to Yankee Station in the Gulf of Tonkin with the carriers, a young supply officer from the aircraft carrier *USS Oriskany (CVA-34)* came aboard the *Chevalier* for a few days of small ship orientation. Such exchange visits were not uncommon, but they were uncommon for supply officers. This particular officer, however, was a friend of LT Al Sherman, the *Chevalier's* Chief Engineer, and that probably had something to do with it. The officer's name was LTJG Frank M. Tunick and his job on board the *Oriskany* was to operate the ship's stores. I met Frank during his visit on the *Chevalier* and we became friends.

Later during the deployment, I went to the *Chevalier* ship's store one day to pick up another carton of Kool Filter Kings. "Sorry, Mr. King, we are out of Kools ... Would you like some Salems?" I was incredulous! The supply officer had let me down? Actually, he had just miscalculated; there were about five other Kool smokers on board. Days went by, and I tried Salems, Newports and even Viceroys (Viceroys are essentially Kools without menthol). The substitutes were not satisfying and I was not a happy sailor.

When a destroyer is assigned carrier escort duty, of course, the carrier is about all there is to look at all day. You essentially rotate between three views of it, from 1000 yards astern, from 2000 yards off the port bow or from 2000 yards off the starboard bow. I cannot remember how many days went by with me staring at the *USS*

Oriskany before the light bulb lit up. I bet the *Oriskany* has Kools! Then it dawned on me that I knew one, and only one, person on board the *Oriskany* — and that one person was Frank Tunick, the Official *USS Oriskany* Keeper of the Kools!

There are several ways to communicate from ship to ship. The most formal way is by Orestes (teletype). But all such communications are official, originating from the commanding officer of the sending ship and addressed to the commanding officer of the receiving ship. Then there are two UHF voice radio circuits, Pri-Tac and Pri-CIC, not quite as formal, but still quite official. Finally, there is good old flashing light, going back to the days of sail. Signalmen often chatted informally about any and every subject from ship to ship with flashing light, and no one seemed to mind.

I decided flashing light was the best way to alert my friend on the *Oriskany* about the *Chevalier's* horrific logistics problem that was severely impairing the concentration of at least one of the *Chevalier's* officers as he went about carrying out his official duties in the conduct of the War in Vietnam. Late that night, after I was fairly sure my captain, the *Oriskany* captain and any admirals aboard *Oriskany* (if any) were asleep, I jotted down the text of a short message: "Person to Person Fm LTJG R. King To LTJG (SC) F. Tunick: BT *CHEVALIER* SHIP'S STORE URGENTLY NEEDS CASE KOOL FILTER KING CIGARETTES BT." I cannot remember what BT means, but it is sort of like the word STOP in an old fashioned telegram. The duty signalman blink blink blinked it off and the *Oriskany* signal bridge receipted for it seconds later.

The following afternoon, I had the JOOD watch on the bridge, and I also had the conn. A big helicopter lifted off *Oriskany's* flight deck and buzzed the *Chevalier*, indicating it had cargo for us. As conning officer, I smartly ordered a turn into the wind and ordered the boatswain's mate to call away the helo transfer detail. This really got Captain Kirk's attention, because our AN/SPS-40 (air search radar) was CasRep'd (broken) for lack of a part and the captain was hoping the helo was bringing the part to us. Also, the promotion board (commander to captain) in Washington was in session and he thought the helo might have an unofficial advance notice of his selection. In any event, he was dead sure the helo had something important!

As soon as the helo finished its drop, I became busy calculating and giving the proper and necessary orders to get the *Chevalier* back into her assigned station. While I was doing that, Captain Kirk picked up the phone (1JV) and talked to the helo transfer detail on the fantail. I could of course only hear his side of the conversation, which went something like this "This is the Captain, what did the helo bring us? ... (a long pause) ... You idiots, that's just the packing carton ... open it up and see what's actually inside ... (another long pause) ... Kool Filter Kings? Kool Filter Kings! .... SLAM!! (*he slammed the phone down in its cradle*)." The captain then went back to his chair and sat down.

As soon as I had the *Chevalier* back in her assigned station, 2000 yards and 45 degrees off the *Oriskany's* starboard bow, I walked up to the captain and stated that I could explain about the Kools. "Kools are my brand and the ship's store ran out ... so I made arrangements to re-stock the ship's store." Captain Kirk just stared at me with a dumbfounded look and then finally said, "Mr. King, you are a lieutenant junior grade on a destroyer in the middle of the ocean in the middle of a war and you can arrange to have your brand of cigarettes delivered to you by vertrep?" I replied, "Captain, if you smoked Kools, you'd understand." At that, he stood up, walked off the bridge and went to his sea cabin, slamming the door behind him.

In the wardroom, the officers ate dinner in two sittings, called logically the first sitting (at 1700) and the second sitting (at 1800). It was Captain Kirk's custom to eat in the wardroom at the second sitting. Protocol calls for the officers to silently sort themselves out and then sit at the one long table by order of rank, with the senior officer at the head of the table, working down both sides by order of rank with the most junior furthest away. I ate in the second sitting that night, and as an ensign or the newest lieutenant j.g., ended up at the bottom of the long table, opposite the captain at the far top end.

Salads were set down, and then the steward came around with the salad dressings, serving the captain first. He looked at the selection and asked, "Where is the bleu cheese?" The steward replied, "Sorry, Captain, we are out of bleu cheese." Now, for the second time that day, the captain was very disappointed. He selected something else and then I noticed him staring at me.

Suddenly, the captain raised his voice and yelled, "Mr. King, you seem to be able to get whatever damn well you want out here, see if you can get me some damn bleu cheese!" All I could do was politely reply, "Aye, aye sir (meaning, I understand the order and I will carry it out)." Late that night, I sent another flashing light message to Frank Tunick, and the next day, there was that same helo again with a ten-pound brick of bleu cheese. How did I do that? I don't know even to this day.

In my next fitness report (in which the captain describes my performance of duty for the Bureau of Personnel) instead of saying something like, "this presumptuous dumb officer exercises poor judgment in the use of Naval resources," there were some words more along the lines of "exercises initiative, imagination and ingenuity in solving difficult logistic problems."

Footnote: On 26 October 1967, while at Yankee Station in the Gulf of Tonkin, the *Oriskany* experienced the worst tragedy of its long service in the US Navy. Fire broke out in the hanger bay forward and engulfed five decks. There were 43 casualties, including LTJG Frank M. Tunick.

SUBKILLER

BY BOB COHEN

Charles F. Adams-class destroyers were designed as true general purpose warships. With their two rapid-firing five-inch gun mounts and an area defense missile system clearly visible, it was obvious they could deal with any threat on the water or in the air. But what about submarines? If you looked closely, you'd notice the AS-ROC eight-cell box, nestled right in between the forward and after smokestacks. This anti-submarine rocket launcher could hurl a homing torpedo or even a nuclear depth-charge at any enemy lurking below. But why would this weapon be located between the stacks, clearly unable to shoot to the front or the rear? Because what you couldn't see on an *Adams*-class ship was the sonar. Unlike most destroyers that had one big transducer in the bow, these destroyers had two: one dome in the bow – and another under the keel, about sixty feet back from the first. What that rig enabled them to do was to send out a powerful ping, and if a target was out there abeam of the sonars, they could then use both domes to triangulate the target's position with deadly precision ... for that almost-hidden ASROC to neatly shoot sideways and drop a big surprise right on top of the unlucky U-boat.

These destroyers didn't carry a helicopter, so in order to fight a submarine they'd have to drive right up on it and get within AS-

ROC range. The ship had a powerful main propulsion plant that allowed it to do just that. With all four boilers lit off, speeds well in excess of thirty knots were no problem. There was one minor detail, though: *Adams*-class destroyers made more noise than a freight train. The ship was designed in the fifties, and while they did incorporate some brand-new technology in the propulsion plant, other technologies were basically unchanged since World War One. Specifically, the myriad of pumps and turbines in the plant, the literally dozens of rotating and reciprocating gadgets needed to steam the ship, were all hard-mounted to the ship's structure. This meant that all the vibration produced by the plant was conducted directly through to the ship's hull, and from there right into the water. Submarines could generally detect an *Adams*-class when it was two or three time-zones away.

So began the great experiment: Could we, the engineers, steam our plant in such a way as to improve the ship's anti-submarine warfare capability? We sure as hell were going to find out. It was an exciting time for us. Although we always knew that we were the primary force behind all of the ship's fighting strength, we never before felt truly connected to it, or tactically involved with it. We just steamed. This was different.

The ship had four boilers and two engines. Each boiler had two forced-draft blowers, each fireroom had three main-feed pumps and three main-feed boosters, and each engineroom had two turbo-generators and a whole bunch of condensate pumps. Normally, nearly every pump was either on the line, or turning over in standby mode. This was to ensure maximum redundancy in case of battle damage or an engineering casualty. Of course, with everything running, a terrific amount of machinery noise was put into the water. So we came up with a plan on how to steam the plant for ASW operations. In theory, it was simple: we would only run the absolute bare minimum amount of equipment necessary to maintain the basic steam cycle. No redundancy, no back up. It was hoped this would be a trade-off for less noise.

We proceeded to a secret Pacific test range where our underwater sound signature would be measured. First, to get a benchmark, we steamed through the range with our normal plant line-up. Just a straight run, nothing fancy. This data was collected and translated into a graphical representation that would clearly display the noise a submarine would hear. The ASW group took this information and prepared a baseline chart.

Now it was Engineering's turn to see if we could make a difference. We *rigged for silent running* – one boiler, one blower, one main feed pump, one booster, et cetera. For a plant designed to run with most of its gear on the line, this was pretty tricky. The plant didn't like it at all, as far as we could tell. Every boiler tech and machinist's mate had his hands full as the plant teetered toward collapse. If you can picture each snipe awkwardly trying to manipulate a set of rabbit-ear antennas to get better television reception, you'll have an idea. The second test run was finally completed without incident, and everyone breathed a sigh of relief. We were just a hair away from the embarrassment of dropping the load the entire time.

That night, we attended a top-secret briefing in the wardroom, given by Frank Hudik, our ASW officer. He had a flipchart with some mysterious graphs standing on an easel. He spoke of things we engineers only dimly understood — sound propagation, decibels, frequencies, and so on. He explained, "If you cut the noise power in half, you only lose three decibels of noise level." Well, during the test we had shut down more than half the equipment we'd normally run. Then he said, "Cutting it in half again loses another 3 dB, so by reducing the noise to one-fourth its previous power level, you've only reduced it 6 dB. To make an appreciable difference in measurable noise would require a reduction on the order of 20-25 dB — or a decrease of a magnitude of 128 to 256 times quieter." We started squirming in our seats. There was only so much equipment that we could shut down. Frank said, "As you can see, this chart is a graphic representation of the ship's sound signature, taken from various points on the range, while steaming steady-state with the standard engineering plant line-up." He continued. "Now gentlemen, *this* graph represents the ship's signature during the second run on the same range, with the special plant line-up that the engineers came up with." There was an uncomfortable pause – he hadn't touched the flipchart. Finally, someone whispered, "You gotta flip the page!" Frank said, "Heh, heh, heh ... No, I don't." Apparently, all of our efforts at silent running were wasted on the submarines, who could still hear us like a freight train – and Frank's attempt at humor was wasted on the captain, who didn't think it was funny at all.

THE BATTLE OF CAT LO

BY DICK KING

During most of January 1968, the *USS Chevalier (DD-805)* was engaged in naval gunfire support in the Saigon River for the US Army. Saigon, although 30 miles inland, is reached by ships via the Saigon River. At the mouth of the river is the old French Indo-Chinese resort town of Vung Tau. In between those two relatively secure cities was a vast area of swamp, jungle and waterways known as the Rung Sat, home of the Viet Cong, and the focus of most of the Chevy's gunfire.

All of our fire was directed by Army spotters, sometimes from small planes or hilltops and sometimes, we eventually realized, somewhat randomly from Army base camps, at suspected Viet Cong encampment areas to deny the VC any rest at night. Our gunfire became a leisurely twenty-four hour activity from what we called Modified Condition Three. In Modified Condition Three, only one gun mount was manned. CIC, the bridge and plot stood port and starboard.

Navigation in the river was tricky. Generally, we fired from anchor, but the Army was frequently asking us to move and it was obvious they knew nothing about our length or displacement. Actually, the *Chevalier* was a very inappropriate ship for this kind of duty, but the Navy didn't have any old river monitors left over from prior wars. In most places, the river was too narrow to turn around, except by sticking the sonar dome in the mud and twisting. The sonar dome was thereby damaged and had to be replaced back in the States.

By the end of the month, everyone was exhausted. Fortunately, January 30, 1968, was the beginning of Tet, the seven-day Vietnamese New Year celebration. Traditionally, even back when the French were fighting, Tet was a period of truce. This coming Tet was to be a continuation of the tradition; by the 29th, we fired only a few rounds in the morning and nothing thereafter.

A few miles from Vung Tau, where the Army had an airfield, the Navy had a small base on a shallow tributary of the river near the town of Cat Lo. It was for Swift boats and PBRs (small fast fiberglass patrol craft) used to patrol the coast and inland waterways of the Rung Sat.

Just prior to Tet, Captain G. G. Ely Kirk got on the radio with the Cat Lo Base Commander to try to arrange for some liberty. The reply from the commander, junior to our captain, was a reluctant "yes," but there was only one Mike boat (utility boat) available, belonging to the *USS Tutuila (ARG-16)*, an ancient combustion engine repair ship converted from a Liberty ship and which sat at anchor in the mouth of the river for years on end during the Vietnam War. The boat could carry only about thirty men and the trip from the *Chevalier's* anchorage to Cat Lo would take over an hour one way. Two nights of liberty were planned for about thirty persons each night. Captain Kirk decreed that he would lead the liberty party on the first night, with one department head, four junior officers, five chief petty officers and the balance, 1st, 2nd and a few 3rd class petty officers, to be selected broadly from all divisions on the basis of merit and performance.

It was late afternoon when the Mike boat from the *Tutuila* arrived alongside. The liberty party boarded and we began the slow twelve-mile trip up the tributary (six miles as the crow flies). Upon arriving at the landing, we split out for the enlisted men's, chief's and officer's clubs, all Quonset huts. The *O* club wasn't much; one big room with a pool table and some chairs, but in the corner there was a bar with hard liquor, beer, and a Vietnamese female bartender. Within a minute, I was enjoying what would be the first of many cold, crisp gin and tonics.

For the next hour or two, we enjoyed our drinks and conversed with the locals. Suddenly, just after dark, we heard gunfire; a siren blew and the lights went out. The base commander told us that the base was under attack. All the local officers rushed out the door, most with sidearms. The base commander told the captain and the one department head to follow him, and they rushed out also. It was New Years Eve Tet, the beginning of what was later to be called the "Tet Offensive," the bloodiest North Vietnamese / Viet Cong offensive of the entire war. The four of us remaining junior officers just stood there wondering what to do.

Then I noticed that the bartender looked like she was closing the bar. I asked her what she was doing and she replied, "I must go to bunker." I told her, "Please leave it open. Put us on the honor system. Leave a box on the bar and we will put our money in it, plus a big tip!" Surprisingly, she agreed and departed!

By now there was gunfire all around us. Looking out the *O* club windows, we could see tracer bullets, flares, mortar rounds, whatever. Slowly it dawned on us that we were in the middle of a land battle and didn't even have one gun between the four of us. While freshening up my drink at the honor bar, I came up with a plan. One of us should go look for the chiefs and petty officers and try to assemble everyone in the same spot. I announced my idea, and fortified with gin, volunteered to do it in the same breath. There were no objections, so I slipped out the door, gin and tonic in hand.

All lights were out, but flares periodically provided enough light to see the various buildings. At the chief's club, I found our chiefs as perplexed at what to do as we were, despite their greater experience. Then I realized their bar had been closed so I invited them to join the junior officers at the *O* club, an invitation quickly accepted.

The trip from the chief's club to the EM club was much longer. I stayed close to buildings and in the shadows. When I got to the EM club, it was dark and absolutely empty. As I stood by the open door pondering what to do next, a Marine came by. I asked him if he had seen about twenty sailors from the ship out in the river. He replied that they had been issued arms and were defending the western base perimeter. I asked him, "Which way is west?" and he pointed away from the tributary by which we had arrived. I said, "Thanks," and headed west into this pitch-black base never before seen. I didn't have a clue how big this base was. By now there were bigger illumination flares over the tributary that helped me find my way. I learned later that the *Chevalier* was firing them. But that's another story. Captain Kirk did his own account of the Battle of Cat Lo, which he wrote and shared with me eight years later.

From the account of Captain G.G. Ely Kirk (paraphrased slightly):
In the midst of all this pleasantry at the *O* club, as I was raising a very dry martini to my lips, all hell broke loose. The total security guaranteed by the base commander was apparently less than total. This, because some of the VC hadn't gotten the word that we were all on a peaceful holiday. Noisy damn rockets or whatever started flying all over the place. Great peaceful holiday!

The lights went out as a siren began to blow. The base commander then furnished me with a pistol belt, holster and Colt revolver. He admonished me that it was loaded, that the safety mechanism was suspect and asked me to follow him. As the crescendo of battle — or whatever the hell it was — increased, I sauntered forth in the murky blackness to sum up the situation. If nothing else, I hoped to find a way to extract my men and myself from this ridiculous situation. It was a mess.

The VC were apparently shooting 37-millimeter rockets across the creek. The base commander had deployed all his Swift boats except one that he wanted for river patrol. Meanwhile, he had men firing flares across the canal to illuminate the opposite bank in order to spot an attacking force. He then ran out of flares. I offered to help him out if he considered himself to be in a real bind. Asked, "How?" I replied, "No problem, Commander, just give me a portable radio and I'll call on the *Chevalier* for help." This he quickly produced and I headed for the signal tower in the center of the small compound. Small arms fire seemed to be everywhere.

After almost being run down by an unlit Jeep, I reached the tower, made radio contact with the *Chevalier* and gave my Executive Officer the geographical grid coordinates for the bank across the creek and ordered him to commence illumination fire. This meant five-inch star shells designed to burst like Fourth of July fireworks over a carefully specified area. I could visualize the XO shaking his head over the whole rather bizarre affair.

The first shot was near perfect and in no time, the whole area was lit up like daylight, with flares drifting down on their tiny parachutes. Shortly thereafter, however, the base commander decided it was too much illumination, illuminating his boats and his base, not just the VC positions. By now it seemed evident that the VC were mostly on the other side of the creek and would have to cross it to overrun the base. In that case, he would take darkness as an advantage and so he asked me to stop. Soon all was dark again and I climbed down to find my way back to the *O* club.

LTJG Dick King's account continues:
I arrived at the west base perimeter in almost no time; it was probably the smallest base I had ever been on. In the dim light, I could see the fence, a cleared area on the other side and a trench inside the fence containing men with weapons every few feet. One man was walking up and down the trench giving instructions and I headed towards him. When I was close, I identified myself and asked who was in charge. He replied, "I am, (something) sergeant (something)," and I jumped down into the trench. Immediately, I was greeted by petty officers from *Chevalier*, all of whom were armed. I then learned that when the siren blew, the Marine sergeant told the petty officers

to follow him to the armory, single file, where each was issued a weapon on the run. Some got M-1s, some got BARs and some even got Thompson submachine guns, without regard to rate, experience or expertise.

The Marine sergeant was almost finished explaining and showing each man how his weapon worked, and in some cases, exchanging some weapons i.e., taking a BAR or Thompson from an electronics technician and exchanging it for an M-1 first arbitrarily issued to a gunner's mate. I asked if everyone was following his instructions, and was told, "Yes sir! They're doing just fine."

Not for the first time that night, I began to ponder what to do next. This sergeant undoubtedly knew more about trench warfare than I could ever hope to learn in a lifetime and I felt absolutely useless. Finally, as I walked down the line of the Chevy petty officers, I told them to follow the sergeant's orders and do whatever he told them. Everyone seemed to be in good spirits and some were clearly hoping that soon there would be some Cong trying to cross the field out front. Then I saw that my gin and tonic glass was empty and decided to go back to the *O* club.

A line from the *O* club to the EM club to the west perimeter wall formed two sides of a triangle. To get back to the *O* club, I decided to complete the triangle by proceeding along a new route. The amount of gunfire seemed to be on the wane. About halfway back, I suddenly heard a voice from above me, "Halt! Who goes there! What's the password?" Looking up, there was a tower, about thirty feet off the ground, the top of which contained a tripod mounted machine gun aimed at my head. I yelled out, "Don't shoot, I'm Lieutenant (j.g.) King from the ship in the river and I don't know the password ... I just came here for some drinks."

A different voice in the tower replied, "Mr. King? Is that you?"

I recognized the voice and replied, "Yes, Donald! What are you doing up there?"

He (BT2 Ronald L. Donald) replied, "I'm with a guy from the base. This is where they put me."

"Hang in there, Donald, I'm going back to the *O* club to make a report."

When I reached the *O* club, Captain Kirk had just returned. I explained what the petty officers were doing and fixed myself another drink, dutifully dropping a few bucks in the honor box. Then I suggested (the captain's version says "insisted") that he visit the troops at the front and volunteered to lead him there. He agreed and we were off again, this time by a new route that would take us safely around Petty Officer Donald's range of fire, which I feared more than the Viet Cong. I was getting good at finding my way around in the dark.

At the front, the captain went down the trench row of petty officers and spoke to each of them. Captain Kirk specifically related in his version of the battle a conversation he had with SM1 Richardson to the effect that "Please let us stick around until we've got a few, this is fun."

Back at the *O* club, there was nothing to do but wait. The captain left to rejoin the base commander. As the night went on, it got quieter and quieter outside. In the morning, we were told to head for the landing where I learned that the petty officers had spent all night in the trench and never fired a shot. Later, I learned that the attack at Cat Lo was deemed to have been diversionary, to keep the Navy base from supporting the Army airfield a few miles away. The Navy base had no casualties or injuries, but the Army base was partly overrun, took some casualties and lost a number of planes.

Although the Battle of Cat Lo may never draw the historical attention as the Battle of Savo Island, Midway or Guadalcanal, it will always remain vivid in my mind, and I am sure, in the memories of those other Chevy sailors who did their part to turn back the Tet Offensive of 1968.

THIS IS NOT A DRILL

BY ROBERT TEGROEN

It was early 1953 when the *USS Small (DDR-838)* headed for Korea. I was in my second year of active duty having gone through a second boot camp because I was a reservist, and then machinist's mate school at Great Lakes. After graduation we got to choose our ship of choice based on our scores. I could have had a battleship, an oiler, even an ammunition ship (no thanks), and three Tin Cans. Of course I chose the Can nearest my home in South Gate, California. It was the *Small* at the Long Beach Naval Shipyard. But I reported to San Diego first, because the whole crew was going through mass training, assignment, and evaluation.

Small had only a skeleton crew while a new bow was being glued on after the original was blown off by a mine off the coast of Korea. Outstanding damage control saved the ship but nine sailors died. *Small* backed down all the way to Japan where a stubby bow was put on for the trip to a shipyard in the States.

We were finally bused to Long Beach to join the ship and soon a recommissioning ceremony was held. Outboard on the port side was the WWII uncompleted destroyer hull that had had its bow removed and grafted onto *Small's* hull. Standing tall, pointing at the sky on the flat weather deck of that ship was the stubby bow, now used as a paint locker. Waste not, want not.

After several months of underway training we got the word we were heading for Korea, one stop, maybe Guam, but not Hawaii, darn. I stood watch on the lower level in the aft engineroom, which was also my GQ station. I forget how many days it was that we headed west but one day the GQ alarm sounded and I thought, "Haven't they done enough drills by now?" But the 1MC then announced "FIRE, FIRE, FIRE, in Compartment (xx,xx,xx) midships storeroom, THIS IS NOT A DRILL!" Well hell's bells Sweet Pea, I think I need to man my battle station. I did so, lighting off the fire & bilge pump on the lower level so as to provide backup firemain pressure. After several hours we found out that the initial attempts to send men down into that compartment, dressed in asbestos suits, had failed. It was just too darned hot. Attempts to use fire hoses with extensions stuck in through that one hatch failed, and finally the whole compartment was flooded right up to the weather deck and hatch. Then when de-watering was attempted with those suction pumps that the navy said would suck up a 2 X 4 but got totally clogged, and Handy Billy pumps got clogged, and nothing could suck up the mixture of tobacco and cereal, a bucket brigade was formed to clean out the mess.

So why the fire? We were on an extended cruise and the supply department brought aboard extra stuff, and a lot of it ended up in that midship storeroom. Only problem was, somebody heaped boxes of cigarettes and Wheatics on top of the main steam cross-connection line. The line was cold when they did it, but once at sea the engineering plant went to cruise control and the forward boilers supplied steam to the aft engineroom, that steam line got heated to 850 degrees of superheat and it was enough to start the fire. That compartment also held the engineering storeroom that contained many small drawers that held itsy-bitsy parts that were now filled with cigarette and cereal goo. Also, the weapons department had all their small arms stored there and most of the wooden stocks had been burned off.

The good side of all this? Well, sitting just above the storeroom on the main deck was the radio electrical supply room. I use this term loosely because I'm only familiar with the knob that turns on my radio, all else is magic. Seems that there were several motor-generator units sitting above the heat and they got fried. So we had to go to a shipyard in Hawaii for several weeks so the radios would work again. Happy Days and Happy Liberty. I got to hone my board surfing at Waikiki Beach and drink legally for the first time (Hawaii drinking age was eighteen, California twenty one). Anybody remember the Merry Go Round Bar in downtown Honolulu?

But all good things must come to an end. We continued on to Korea and Japan where I must admit I was a naughty boy.

YOU CATCH A CARRIER BY SNEAKIN' UP ON 'EM

BY KEN DANDURAND

The exercise called for the *USS South Carolina (DLGN-37)* to sneak up and launch a missile attack on the aircraft carrier *USS Nimitz (CVN-68)*. Not an insurmountable task, but difficult to say the least. It is the sort of challenge that makes Commanding Officers giddy. It is the kind of task that can make the crew proud and much more solidified with the ship, its abilities, and its leadership.

The captain laid out a plan to his officers and they, in turn, directed the appropriate crewmembers, instructing them on what was expected of them. The shipfitters acquired two-and three-inch pipe in forty-foot lengths. The electricians procured running and deck lights. The deck crew broke out the gear that they needed. The sonar, radar and fire control people made their preparations. The engineers made preparations to have the nuclear power plant slow down and steam like a boiler-operated ship.

Everything hinged first, on what the enemy could see and not what it detected and second, on the fact that carriers rarely change course. The ocean is a big place. On its surface sail many ships, ships of every conceivable type. More ships than one can imagine, especially at night.

The shipfitters welded the running and deck lights on the ends of the forty-foot pipes. The electricians wired them. The shipfitters and boatswain's mates rigged the pipes over the sides of the ship and up in the air. More lights were added on the main deck. The CO, the XO and the First Lieutenant inspected the work. All looked good.

By sundown, the Navigator had his coordinates. The course and speed were calculated for an early morning intercept. The timing was fine-tuned and everything was double-checked. The sonar men turned off the sonar. All radar was turned off with the exception of the AN/SPS-10 and the Loran. Radio silence was observed. All fire control equipment was de-energized. Finally, the ship changed course and the ship's lights were turned off and the "new" lights were turned on.

The mighty American warship *South Carolina* had now become a merchant vessel, steaming south-southeast along the eastern seaboard at ten knots. The new running lights changed the beam from sixty one feet to ninety feet. The ship's length appeared to have changed from five hundred and ninety-six feet to about six hundred and thirty feet. In addition, no warship would steam around with all those deck lights on.

All through the night the people on the bridge and in CIC listened to the radios and watched the radar screen and the lights in the coal black darkness outside. There was no moon on this night.

The *Nimitz* had her planes out. She was searching for any signatures or radio traffic. She was searching everywhere! We could hear on the radio traffic when someone would ask about a contact bearing 352 degrees (us). Soon a Harrier was hovering just off our port side. We looked for it but could not see it. It had its lights turned off, but we could sure hear it. It just hovered there for about two minutes and then took off. Then we could hear on the radio "Unidentified ship at such and such appears to be a merchant vessel." Everyone on the bridge and CIC burst out in cheers. Cheers which the CO did shortly curtail.

This scene repeated itself a couple of times during the night. Each time the Harrier would come over to re-verify the contact and would go into its hovering mode with lights off and just hover there and watch the ship. At other times, jets would just fly over.

It was now 0400 and the *Nimitz* was getting antsy about where the *South Carolina* was located. First light was at 0600 sharp.

She should be somewhere close. Again the radio traffic questioned the contact and again the planes flew over.

At approximately 0500 the *Nimitz* went to flight quarters and launched jets. The captain of the carrier was no dummy either. He may be surrounded by peacetime shipping along a friendly coast, but there was a threat out there somewhere, and the planes would find it sooner or later.

As 0600 approached, everyone on the SoCar got nervous. The approach had been flawless. The timing appeared to be right on the money. We were undetected thus far. Even the captain's eyes looked like a kid who was about to open a big red present.

All appropriate personnel were up and making their preparations. The fire controlmen were bringing their gear up. The radarmen were standing by. The radiomen had a finger on the radio switch. The captain was now watching the plot board, radar screen and listening to a steady input from his CIC personnel. Every few seconds he would look behind him. The door to CIC from the bridge was open and he had a clear view of the horizon. Several times the jets flew over and everyone knew they were *really* antsy now. No warship captain would be caught in the open at daybreak!

As first light appeared, the captain held the radio microphone in his hand and nodded. We had radar, we had fire control, and we had radio. We had the first transmission of the day from our CO: "MIKE, MIKE, MIKE." We could picture the Tarters leaving the rail and streaming across the sky. This was followed by about a ten second delay and then the sound of two jets flying stem to stern fifty feet above our mast. WHOOOSH! WHOOOSH!

SITTING OUT GRENADA

BY BOB COHEN

Our high-tech, nuclear-quality 1200-psi boilers were still just boilers. As such, they needed occasional cleaning to stay healthy. We cleaned them the same way anybody ever cleaned boilers, by periodically blowing steam all over the boiler's gizzards with some decidedly low-tech gadgets called soot-blowers — rotating steam nozzles sticking into the boiler that we manually swiveled around by means of some primitive chain-and-sprocket thing. One day, while "blowing tubes" as it was known, we broke one of the soot-blowers. Shit, *that* never happened before … and try as we might, we couldn't fix it.

Next thing you know, I'm up on the bridge trying to explain it to the captain, who wants to know the status of his boiler. "Captain, the boiler's fine, we just broke the soot-blower, that's all." For some reason, he didn't like that answer. "I understand you broke the soot-blower; is the boiler up or down?" I said, "Well, right now, it's down, but you can steam it if you want." He seemed satisfied with that. Then I added, "For a while, anyway."

"What do you mean, 'for a while?' Is that boiler up or down, mister?"

"It's down now, but — I guess it's up. You can steam it, we just can't clean it." Always pragmatic, I tried explaining that the boiler could steam a certain amount of hours between firesides, and I recommended that we just leave the boiler in stand-by until we pulled into port. That way, if we needed it, we could light it off and use it for a while. We could always take it out of service afterwards. Maybe the captain was in a bad mood over something else, but I got yelled at a bit and was ordered to take that boiler out of service — now.

A few days later, we pull into San Diego and commence to take the boiler apart. Everyone's sitting in the wardroom that afternoon as the engineers hook up the telephone and shore services. The TV comes on. They're showing some type of war map with all kinds of arrows and diagrams. Must be a documentary of some sort. The announcer says, "Today, US forces blah, blah, blah …" As we gradually realized we were watching the local evening news, the command duty officer mumbled, "Uh, somebody better go get the Skipper …"

Since we were less than 24 hours' transit from the war zone

via the Panama Canal, it was then officially designated as my personal fault that we were unable to participate in the Grenada invasion over a CasRep'd boiler with a busted soot-blower.

FUN WITH PMS

(PLANNED MAINTENANCE SYSTEM)

CARL SIMS

As the USS *Basilone (DD-824)* returned from Vietnam in the summer of 1966, she had been relieved of her .50 caliber machine guns. However, the ship still had a .30 caliber machine gun, a couple of Thompson submachine guns and assorted pistols and rifles.

I had been aboard about two years when the gunner's mates had to PM the small arms locker, meaning every small arm the ship had needed to be fired, disassembled, cleaned and re-assembled and certified as having been operationally tested. As part of this PM, the captain decided to qualify all weapons officers on all of the small arms, including the Thompson and the .30 cal machine gun. Or at least he acquiesced to their request to become qualified on these weapons.

Chief Gunner's Mate Smith and GMG3 Brown proceeded to take all the small arms up to the DASH hanger. Pistol qualifications went without a hitch. Now came the real work that the gunner's mates had to do ... fire the Thompson and the .30 caliber machine gun. Well, this was what every officer had been waiting for. It was also the one thing that the gunner's mates wanted to do too. After all, they were GUNNER'S MATES!

Here I must insert a characteristic of the Thompson: During full automatic fire, the muzzle would climb away from the target and had to be compensated for by the shooter.

Chief Smith gave each of the officers the Thompson in turn, handed each a 20-round clip, instructed them about the muzzle climb and then observed as they inserted the clip, pulled back the bolt, disengaged the safety, braced themselves against the recoil and fired at flotsam which the ship was passing by. After the officers were finished, Chief Smith found that there were sufficient clips left to allow him to fire a clip and for both of his rated gunner's mates to also qualify.

GMG3 Brown was a kid who couldn't have weighed 110 pounds soaking wet. He was the cocky sort and was proud of having been recently promoted and placed in charge of the weapons locker. His cockiness almost proved my personal undoing.

Chief Smith handed the last clip to Brown and admonished him to follow the same procedure that everyone else had used. Brown was grinning from ear to ear as he took the Thompson. His "expert" hands placed the clip into the weapon and he eagerly released the safety, drew back the bolt and chambered his first round. He fired a single shot into a clump of seaweed perhaps 100 feet away with an accuracy unseen from any of the other qualifiers. Proud of his accomplishment, he then fired a 5-round burst at the same target. The effect this time was a little unsettling — the first two rounds fell on the target, but the others fell further away in a line to be expected from the muzzle climb. Still grinning, he took aim rather casually and turned the Thompson loose!

I saw the muzzle climb to the sky and Brown began to fall over backward with his finger still firmly gripping the firing Thompson. I was paralyzed. When the firing stopped, Brown was on his back, arms over his head holding the now-empty Thompson pointed directly toward me. I was the only one standing up. Chief Smith was dragging himself out of the netting of the flight deck, all of the officers were getting up from the flight deck mad as hell, and Brown just lying there with an astonished look on his face and the Thompson still pointed right at me.

This little incident caused the testing of the .30 caliber machine gun to take place on the lower weather deck, barrel firmly lashed to a stanchion and unable to move.

APRIL 14TH

MY LONGEST DAY

BY GARY WHITE

April 14th, 1969 started out routinely enough. Reveille at 0600, muster at 0800 and then turn to. *USS Mahan (DLG-11)*, having been in port at Yokosuka, Japan for a planned 21-day maintenance period since March 28^{th,} was on a four section watch, each section working for three days and off the fourth. Monday, the 14th was my section's day off and most of the us hit the beach immediately following muster. While many of my shipmates headed straight for the "Honcho," the area just outside the main gate of Yokosuka Naval Station filled with bars, cheap gift shops and a few small cafes, several of us decided to take the train to Yokohama and visit the shopping district before joining other members of the crew in what would probably be our last chance for some serious partying for several weeks. Little did we know at the time just how true that prophesy was.

After a long evening of barhopping, I returned to the ship just before midnight. Up the gangway, a salute to the officer of the deck and straight down to my berthing compartment took only a few short minutes and into my rack for some welcome rest even less. After what seemed like a very short night, the compartment lights suddenly came on and the division first class petty officer, STG1 Baca, was shaking my bunk. "Let's go, White. Get dressed and muster on the fantail. We need to retrieve the fathometer from the SRF shop on the pier." Glancing at my watch confirmed my suspicions; I had been asleep for exactly 14 minutes! "Hey, Baca. Why are we going after the fathometer when it isn't our gear and in the middle of the night, no less?" The reply woke me up in a hurry. The squadron had been put on 24-hour alert to depart for the Sea of Japan and begin search and rescue operations for a Navy EC-121 aircraft. The reconnaissance flight, assigned to Squadron VQ-1 out of Atsugi Naval Air Station, Japan, had been flying over international waters parallel to the Korean coast when it was attacked and shot down by North Korean MiG-15's. *Mahan* needed the fathometer for navigation in the shallow straits we would have to traverse en route to the Sea of Japan and our group had been charged with returning it to the ship from the repair shop and seeing that it was placed in the chartroom on the O-4 level behind the bridge.

By 0330 we had the fathometer back aboard ship. Now came the next challenge, how to get a 400-lb. piece of equipment up four decks without the assistance of the crane which had taken it off the ship. After almost two hours of man-handling up four outside ladders, the fathometer was finally back in its rightful place. By this time, however, the ship was on 2-hour alert and all crew members still on liberty had been recalled. At 0600 all required personnel were back aboard but unlike *USS Sterett (DLG-31)* which departed at 0600, *Mahan* was held until 1500 on the 15th. When we departed Yokosuka to meet *Sterett*, *USS Dale (DLG-19)* and *USS Henry W. Tucker (DD-875)*, eighty enlisted and three officers of *Sterett* were embarked aboard *Mahan*. They had been left behind earlier that morning.

After my ordeal with the fathometer I ate breakfast and reported to my duty station, the sonar shack. Unfortunately, lighting-off and calibrating our sonar equipment took several more hours and as luck would have it, I also was part of the aft line-handling party. At 1620 on Tuesday, the 15th of April, 1969 I was finally able to crawl behind the tactical sonar computer console and curl up on a life preserver for a short nap. I had just completed a 14-minute night and a 34-hour day. It would be May 27th before the next liberty call.

Footnote: The loss of the thirty Navy and one Marine Corps aircrew who were aboard the EC-121 from Squadron VQ-1 has been cited as the single worst "Killed in Action" casualty of the Cold War.

Hmm…That's Odd

FARRAGUT / COONTZ CLASS
Length: 512' Displacement: 4853 tons 10 built, in service 1960-1993

STG3 Gary White
WA Division, USS Mahan (DLG-11) 1968-69

LTJG Mike Snyder
Missile Division, USS Coontz (DLG-9) 1973-74

OS2 (SW) Jack Dineen
OI Division, USS King (DDG-41) 1978-81

NASTY JACK

BY DAVE CARLSON

Nasty Jack was a specialist from DATC/FMAG, which was the precursor to NAVSEA. He specialized in the Mark 1 Able Fire Control computer. The Mk 1A computer was not a computer by the modern definition of the word. It was a mass of gears, cams, and shafts of every possible type. The only things electrical about it were the 60-Hz motors that drove those gears. It was built by Ford and was actually called a *Rate Keeping Machine*. Despite its origin in the late '30s, it was perfectly capable of tracking any target up to 500 kts. Beyond that, it just couldn't function. Its designers never conceived of targets that could exceed that speed. Being mechanical, it needed occasional adjustments to stay accurate.

While the Fire Controlmen of the *McKean* were perfectly capable of routine maintenance of the Mk 1A, no one on board, or probably in the squadron, would have been able to make complex adjustments. We just weren't trained for it. That's when we called DATC/FMAG for support.

That's where Jack came in.

Jack was a retired Fire Controlman who had served aboard the *USS West Virginia (BB-48)* from Pearl Harbor on. He was old and as cranky and foul-tempered as they came. No one messed with him, NO ONE. Even the officers steered clear. Jack was more than willing to remove anyone's head. He was too old and too salty to tolerate anyone's crap. He was also far too valuable to ever be fired. There was no one who could do what he could with that computer on the West Coast. So you didn't cross Jack. He would eat you alive. The only one who approached was our captain, CDR Larry Smith. Jack liked the captain, and the captain liked him. More than that, they respected each other.

I had never met him before, but the other guys had and were very happy to let me deal with him while they scattered. Joe Herr, my senior third-class filled me in as best he could and then split saying, "Good luck!" At the time FTG3 Dave Graebner was assigned to the Mk 1A so he would work with Jack when he came aboard. "Does it have to be me? He scares the hell out of me!" said Dave. "Yep, you're the guy. You've been doing computer maintenance for the last three months, so you're it," I said.

I met Jack on the quarterdeck. He was there at 0700 sharp. He smelled like he'd already killed a six-pack, but was razor sharp. As we headed for gun plot, I told him we would do everything we could to help him and really appreciated his help. "Just gimme your best computer guy, what I need when I want it, keep plot clear, and we'll get along fine," he growled. When we entered plot, I introduced him to Dave and shooed everyone else out. They didn't have to be told twice. We had just started when the captain poked his head in and asked Jack if he'd like to come to the wardroom for some coffee. Jack said, "I'll be right up, Captain, just let me get these guys started first. I hope you've something better than coffee for me to drink." The captain said he could manage that, and left. Jack gave us some instructions and then took off for the wardroom. I told Dave that I was pretty sure that if he just did what was asked, when he was asked, things would be okay. We did the things Jack had told us to do, and then waited for him to come back.

Jack came back in about fifteen minutes. He and Dave went to work. As long as you jumped and didn't ask a lot of questions, he was happy. Mostly he would make an adjustment and then have Dave run a test. I helped when I could, but tried to stay out of the way and do my own work unless asked. He taught Dave a lot of tricks and they were done by noon.

He talked a little about being on the Wee Vee. He told us a little about Pearl Harbor and the rebuild she went through, and the march across the Pacific. At lunch, he headed for the wardroom. That was what the captain had wanted, to invite him to lunch, after they had had some coffee. After lunch, he had Dave run a few more tests. When he was satisfied, he packed up and I escorted him back to the quarterdeck and saw him off. We were all pretty impressed with his sea service.

I departed the *McKean* a few months later, my active duty completed. FTG2 Larry Pallozola took over as Division LPO. Larry related the following to me about an encounter he had with Jack: "It was rumored that Jack had had a heart attack. Although I still had chew marks on my ass from last time I saw him, I felt bad for him. Also felt bad for any Seventh Fleet ship that might need help on their Mk 1 A, because when it came to servicing them, there was none better than Jack. At any rate, we were scheduled for DATC availability, and someone was coming over to work on our Mk1 A. Had no idea who it would be. I was in gun plot when someone (Herr?) came in with a look of terror on his face, and said, 'It's Nasty Jack! Just saw him coming aboard.' I was afraid the thumper would have taken the wind out of his sails, and I expected to see a broken and humbler man, then the door to gun plot flew open. There he stood, with clear and fiery eyes, and smelling like a distillery. 'You, you, and you, get the fuck out! Where's Petty Officer Graebner?'

'I'll get him,' I replied as I ran out."

For good or for bad, he was still his feisty old self.

I was happy to hear Jack hadn't changed. Jack was truly Old Navy. A hard-living, hard-drinking, foul-mouthed, cantankerous old son-of-a-swab. He had more salt water in his socks than all the rest of us put together. He was a Pearl Harbor veteran who had seen the entire war, cover to cover. Ol' Nasty Jack was a hell of a guy.

MEASURE ONCE, CUT TWICE

BY DAVE HOOD

Part of my ASROC PMS (No, no, no! PMS in Navyspeak stood for Preventive Maintenance System) required that I periodically open up the panels to all of my electronic components and clean selected terminals with a Q-tip dipped in isopropyl alcohol. The PMS card that told me when, where and how to do the chore even listed the NSN — Naval Stock Number— so that I could order isopropyl alcohol in pint bottles and Q-tips by the handful.

When my supply of isopropyl alcohol started to run low I filled out the forms to get more (always re-order *before* you run out rather then after). About a month went by when the word was passed that I was needed in the Supply Office. "Hood, you have a parts package on the pier."

"What's it doing on the pier?"

"It's too big to bring aboard."

"Too big? What is it?"

"Just go get it off the pier, will ya?"

At the end of the brow was a pallet with a tag on it that said, "HOOD WW01 DD-784." Sitting on top of the pallet was a 55-gallon drum of isopropyl alcohol! Holy crap! A lifetime supply of rubbing alcohol. I wanted one pint. What the hell happened here? I checked the stenciled stock number on the drum and compared it to the numbers on the PMS card and on the paperwork that I had filled out to order it. The numbers were off by one digit.

I went back to the Supply Office and told them that an error had been made and that we need to send this drum back. They all gave me a blank stare and then, as if on cue, every single SK, SH and DK in the office burst out laughing. "You want to send something back? Send it back? Are you nuts? The Navy supply system doesn't want a damn thing sent back! Who the hell do you think you are dealing with, Sears and Roebuck? Send it back? Get the hell out of our office!"

A week went by before the word was passed, "GMT2 Hood. Lay to the wardroom." The CDO wanted to tell me that the city's Fire Marshal had just been out here and when he saw that 55-gallon drum of alcohol he just about had a shit-fit and I needed to get it off of his pier pronto. I rigged up the over-the-side handling boom, the one we used to bring ASROC missiles and torpedoes onto the ship, and hoisted the drum and its pallet aboard. I stashed it over by Rail Storage.

A week later the word was passed, "GMT2 Hood. Lay to the wardroom." The ASWO let me know that the XO saw my drum and wanted to know why I was storing fifty-five gallons of volatile liquid on the weather deck. I then was told to do something with it.

I decided that if I can't return it I might as well start using it up. My pint bottle was starting to get low anyway. I opened the seal and then realized that there was no practical way to pour into a one-pint bottle from a 55-gallon drum. Two gallons later my pint bottle was now full. I tracked down the ETs, FTs, EMs, RMs and STs and inquired if they needed any isopropyl alcohol. They all said that they could use a pint or two. Do they have their own bottles? A few did but some didn't. Six gallons later I had successfully gotten rid of three more pints.

"Hey Hood. I heard down in the hole that you are giving away free alcohol."

"You just need your own bottle."

"Got one right here."

He took an empty flask of Jim Beam out from his coat pocket.

"Get out of here!"

Another week went by. "GMT2 Hood — Quarterdeck." It was the Weapons Officer. "Hood, you *have* to get that barrel off this ship. I don't care how you do it but when we're getting underway next week and when we pull in, Staff is holding an inspection. It has to be gone by then."

"Aye, aye, sir. We wouldn't be having a fantail shoot scheduled, would we?"

With the SelRes aboard, we got underway and steamed for the Pond. Once in the Pacific, the ship slowed to a crawl. I dropped the starboard-side lifelines and pushed my now forty-five gallons of isopropyl alcohol over the side. I hurriedly put the top lifeline in place and ran to the fantail. GMG2 Donnie Hodges was loading a belt of 7.62mm ammo into the feed tray of an M-60 GPMG. "Hey, Donnie! Let me shoot first. It's my drum."

"Screw you! It's my gun."

While we were bickering back and forth, GMG2 Dave Baker picked up the 60 and let loose with *bangbangbangbangbangbang-bangbangbangbangbangbangbangbangbangbangbangbangbangbang bangbang!* Every fifth round was a tracer and maybe fifty rounds were let loose before the drum exploded in a fireball.

A few months later one of the Supply Clerks found me, "Hey Hood, you signed for a barrel of alcohol a while ago. The empty drum is a turn-in item. Make sure they get it back, okay?"

I REMEMBER CARMEN'S VELVET BREASTS

BY ARNOLD HOFMANN

Once upon a time, many years ago, before draconian rules of political correctness, before everyone was offended by everything, there was an Executive Officer on the *USS Reeves (DLG-24)*, Commander Daniel Richardson, who owned a picture of a beautiful lady. She was painted on black velvet, which coincidentally showed a beautiful perky bare breast. I knew her as Carmen.

Now it came to pass that the *Reeves* was in port at Subic Bay, PI when CDR Richardson received orders to detach immediately and to report to his next duty station. As he was leaving the ship, he stopped to say goodbye to LCDR Dave Ruble, the Supply Officer, and gave him his beautiful velvet painting of Carmen as a gift. Ruble, recognizing the sentimental value of this painting, kept it safe during the remainder of the deployment.

Several months later when the *Reeves* returned to her home port in Pearl Harbor, Hawaii, LCDR Ruble happened to inquire at the Supply Center Household Goods Office, whether or not CDR Richardson's household goods had been shipped yet. As luck would have it, all of his possessions were crated and in the warehouse awaiting shipment. With the help of the officer in charge of the household goods section, they opened one of the crates and inserted Carmen. Just imagine the surprise and delight of CDR Richardson and his wife when they moved into their new home.

As time passed, CDR Richardson found a way to have Carmen rejoin LCDR Ruble, who found a way to have Carmen returned to CAPT Richardson, who returned her to CDR Ruble. Now CDR Ruble flinched when it came time to send Carmen back to Rear Admiral Richardson. After all, CDR Ruble was himself trying to amount to something. The cad then summarily abandoned Carmen. He not only abandoned her, but sold her to Mr. Wilson Mebane, a chemist at the Manchester Fuel Depot, for $5, to seal the deal forever.

About five years later, when I was the Commander of the Manchester Fuel Depot, I heard the story about Carmen. I was so moved by the story that I called Wilson into the office and asked him if he still had Carmen. He said he had sold her to one of the laborers a few years ago for $10 but he thought that the laborer might still have her. I told him I wanted to buy her back. With a big grin and an obvious chance to make a buck, Wilson said he would make some inquiries. He later reported back with a big smile and said that he could buy her back, but she wouldn't be cheap. After some negotiations, I bought Carmen back for $20.

Now about that time, Commander Ruble had been selected for Captain and his new assignment was to be Commanding Officer, Navy Petroleum Office. I had previously been Executive Officer there and knew most of the people. I sent Carmen with a letter from the Manchester Fine Arts Commission telling how the commission was all puffed up with pride over Ruble's promotion and asked to have this painting presented to him for his promotion to Captain. Carmen was presented to him at a meeting for all employees.

As timing and coincident happen, Captain Ruble finished his tour and was reassigned to Commander Surface Force Atlantic Fleet in Norfolk, Virginia. I happened to be in Washington DC and stopped to say hello to my friend Captain Jan Carstanjen, the new Commanding Officer of Navy Petroleum Office. As I was leaving the office, I noticed the edge of something familiar sticking out from behind a book cabinet and lo and behold there was Carmen, abandoned again. I told Jan the story and took her with me. I quickly arranged to have her sent to my friend Commander Gary Cornelison in Norfolk where he had her hung on the office wall to greet Captain Ruble on his first day in his new job. Mission accomplished, but of course this time I disavowed any knowledge of Carmen's whereabouts.

A couple of years later I retired from the Navy and I was back in Everett, Washington when a package arrived at my office. Guess what, Carmen was sent back to me to adorn a new club house that I had built. She was as pretty as ever but I knew in my heart that she would never be mine.

As talent and luck would have it, Captain Ruble was promoted to Rear Admiral and his first admiral's job was Deputy Commander, Naval Supply Systems Command, Washington DC. You already know what happened next, but it wasn't easy. Very few people are willing to mess with an admiral's sense of humor. It took some searching to find someone willing to deliver the goods. Captain Ralph Collins agreed to get Carmen on the wall of the Admiral's new office when he arrived on his first day of work. Mission accomplished.

When Admiral Ruble subsequently tried to return Carmen to me again, she was lost in transit. All we have left is a photograph and our memories. She was a high-mileage babe, but we loved her. Carmen, if you're still out there, we miss you. Please come back.

A MATCH OF WITS BETWEEN LTJG RICHARD H. KING AND REAR ADMIRAL ELMO R. ZUMWALT, LATER TO BE CHIEF OF NAVAL OPERATIONS

(ZUMWALT THAT IS, NOT KING)

BY DICK KING

My local newspaper reported that Admiral Elmo R. Zumwalt, Chief of Naval Operations from 1970 to 1974, died January 2, 2000 from complications following cancer surgery. The article included a summary of his flag rank career, including his role in deciding to use Agent Orange in Vietnam and his decisions to permit facial hair, to allow sailors to carry civilian clothes on board ships, to combat racial discrimination and to allow women to serve on board Navy ships. He was also a major player in the debates concerning the *high-low mix*, the strategy of having some lower-cost ships mixed in with more capable and expensive ones. He is often called the "father of the *Knox*-class frigate," a dubious honor in my opinion.

Inaptly referred to as the "fast frigates" of the 1970s that were a third slower than World War Two destroyers, they were not the only thing he and I disagreed about. He also didn't like the standard destroyer engineering department organization chart. Since the time steam propulsion replaced sails, every Navy ship had a Chief Engineer together with some assistant engineering officers. After World War Two, on a destroyer, there would usually be two assistant engineering officers. One was called the DCA (Damage Control Assistant) and the other was called the MPA (Main Propulsion Assistant).

The DCA name was somewhat of a misnomer because no reference was made to his day-to-day duties of maintaining all of the ship's auxiliary engineering systems, including electrical systems, interior communications, refrigeration, ventilation and air conditioning, compressed air, plumbing systems, *ad infinitum*. If a light bulb burned out on the mast, or a toilet didn't flush in the forward crew's head, it was the DCA's problem. The DCA also served as R Division Officer. This division was a medley of ratings, including electricians,

IC electricians, machinist mates (for air-conditioning and refrigeration), enginemen (emergency diesel generators, boat engine, portable fire pumps), damage controlmen (damage control equipment) and shipfitters (welders, sheet metal and plumbers). The typical WWII-designed *Sumner/Gearing* destroyer had an allowance for about 30 men in R Division, and as a practical matter, usually actually had about 25.

If Admiral Zumwalt had any concern about the DCA's duties, however, he never told me about them. But he did have concerns about the MPA's duties, as I was to learn. On *Sumner/Gearing* destroyers, the MPA had two separate divisions — B Division, consisting of boilermen who made the steam, and M Division, consisting of machinist mates who took B Division's steam and converted it into mechanical energy to propel the ship through the water and to generate electricity. Both M and B divisions had allowances of about 30 men each, or about 25 each in actuality. Thus the MPA was Division Officer to somewhere between 50 and 60 men, as it varied from time to time, the most of any junior officer on the ship! The MPA also had two different Leading Chiefs which could be a blessing or a problem, depending on each ship's unique personnel situation.

M Division and B Division have a long tradition of not getting along very well. They constantly argued over almost everything, stole each other's tools and blamed the other division if something went wrong with the main plant. I thought the MPA billet was a brilliant idea, because the MPA could also serve as the referee between the two divisions, without having to involve the chief engineer in every petty dispute between them. I became the MPA on the *USS Chevalier (DD-805)* in January of 1967.

Elmo R. Zumwalt made Rear Admiral (lower half) in the mid 1960s, at age 44 the youngest ever, and in due course he was assigned as COMCRUDESFLOT something (commander of a cruiser and destroyer flotilla, the number of which I have forgotten). Flotillas are kind of hard to describe, especially those of the 1960s. They were a collection of ships for certain administrative purposes and were composed of squadrons, which in turn were composed of divisions. It was a very artificial and contrived arrangement, because flotillas never went to sea together. But then, neither did squadrons or divisions. I think flotillas were just a place to park very junior rear admirals while they did their OJT (on-the-job training) while squadrons and divisions were billets to house senior captains waiting for retirement. I doubt if anyone in those days, except maybe the captain, could tell you the names of many of the other ships that were also in our flotilla.

But I did know that the *Chevalier* was in Admiral Zumwalt's flotilla. The reason I knew that is because we had a flotilla party one night at the North Island Officer's Club in San Diego and I had to go through the receiving line where Admiral and Mrs. Zumwalt stood at the end of the line. I remember it was hot and I had to wear that white uniform that had the stiff collar that you couldn't button by yourself. In fact, it was real hard to button for someone else. After the receiving line, I do not recall speaking to the admiral again that night, but I do remember having a nice conversation with Mrs. Zumwalt. She was a White Russian refugee from the Communist Revolution that the admiral had met somewhere in the orient and she still spoke with a heavy Russian accent.

My next encounter with the admiral was during a personnel inspection in which he was the inspecting officer. As usual, the Engineering Department was assembled on the fantail. R Division was on the starboard side facing to port, M Division was near the counter facing forward and B Division was on the port side facing to starboard. The brow was to starboard, so R Division was inspected first. Then the admiral turned to M Division and I saluted him while reciting the personnel statistics, i.e., number of men assigned, number on watch and number of all others accounted for or in the Tijuana jail, etc. I was of course very nervous and sweating. I believe this was the first time I ever presented a division to an admiral. But M Division did pretty good and soon it was over.

Then the trouble began. As soon as the admiral and I saluted each other again, signaling the end of the M Division inspection, I did a parade ground maneuver which seemed to confuse him. Really, all I did was a few quick steps around the corner to stand in front of B Division, ready to go through the whole routine again! He didn't seem very interested in my B Division statistics, and even interrupted me. "Are you telling me, Mr. King, that you are both the M Division Officer and the B Division Officer?" I had to answer truthfully, "Yes sir," and indeed, I thought that was the way it was on all Navy destroyers, everywhere? No one had told me that there were two schools of thought on that, or that the admiral was from the other school.

As part of a special on television the other night, they showed a clip from the famous *kitchen debate* between then-Vice President Richard Nixon and Prime Minister Nikita Khrushchev, in which they argued about who had the better system, the US or the USSR. The clip reminded me of what happened next on the *Chevalier* fantail, only the debate was between the admiral and me. He argued that I couldn't carry out my duties as Division Officer properly, with so many men, and I argued back why I thought it was a good system and why I thought I was doing a good job despite the numbers. Neither the captain nor the chief engineer jumped in to help me although they were both standing right there, watching and listening.

Finally, Admiral Zumwalt said, "Well, let's get on with it," and we started down the ranks of B Division. By now, I was really sweating. When we were almost done, we came to the next sailor, a fireman apprentice. I had first met this particular sailor the day before the inspection; that was the day he came on board the ship to report for duty. Perhaps feeling a bit peeved about losing the *fantail debate*, as I will always call it, Admiral Zumwalt suddenly turned to me and asked, "Mr. King, what is this sailor's name?" He thought he had me!

Under less stressful circumstances, I might have been able to think of it, or I would have explained that he was brand new and I had forgotten. But this was becoming very stressful. I looked at another fireman we had already passed, whose name was Parker and replied to the admiral, "Parker, sir." The reply just kind of blurted out on its own without my brain engaging, but as my neurons began to work, I realized I was in deep do-do now and sinking deeper by the nanosecond.

The admiral then turned to the sailor in question and asked, "Parker, how long have you been on board this ship and how do you like it so far?" I knew now my goose was cooked and a brief image of NAVCOMSTA ADAK flashed in my mind. Naval Communications Station, Adak, Alaska, was the worst duty station in the Navy, where they sent people who didn't quite qualify for the Portsmouth Naval Prison, but were very, very close.

Almost without hesitation, the misidentified fireman apprentice answered simply "This is my second day sir, and I like it fine so far." The admiral said, "Very good, Parker," and we proceeded on down the row. Then it was suddenly over and the admiral headed forward down the port side towards the next division. I had gotten away with it!

My legs were like rubber and there was enough sweat under my cover to fill the deaerating feed tank, but I managed to apologize profusely to both Parker (the real one) and the brand-new fireman apprentice who had kept his cool and hadn't corrected his name. I don't think I ever saw Admiral Zumwalt again, but years later, after he became CNO and I was then in the reserves, whenever another "Z-Gram" (a general message explaining some change in personnel policy) came out, it brought back some not-so-fond memories of the great fantail debate of 1967.

Footnote:

Lower half and *upper half* identified two different pay grades for two-star rear admirals. This subject is a bit confusing, so bear with me. Originally, we had commodores (one star), rear admirals (two stars), vice admirals (three stars) and admirals (four stars). Then, in WWII, there was a sudden need for large numbers of desk-bound flag officers to be inducted into the Navy directly from industry or the merchant marine. To differentiate between these 90-day "flag wonders" and the Annapolis graduates of the same rank serving at sea, the civilians were called commodores but the regulars were allowed to use the title *rear admiral* and got to use two stars even though they should have had but one.

After the war, the commodores were separated from active service and the rank was phased out. This really pissed off the Army and the Air Force, because they had one-star brigadier generals who were actually the same rank or even senior to some of the two-star rear admirals in the Navy. This also created havoc at White House and State Department dinners! Sometimes a brigadier general would be seated at the same table as the Assistant Ambassador from Outer Mongolia, while a rear admiral, junior to that general, might be seated with the Ambassador from Norway. It was all very confusing to the poor ladies who planned these things.

Finally, in the 1980s, Congress forced the Navy to reinstitute the one-star Commodore rank. This lasted for only a few years, and then the Navy talked Congress into letting them re-adopt the title rear admiral for new flag officers, but unlike before, we now had one-star rear admirals and two-star rear admirals, depending on their seniority! See, its really very simple!

SKIPPER

BY DAVE HOOD

Before I actually enlisted in '75, I learned all I needed to know about the navy by reading *Captain Storm* comic books. Captain Storm, you may remember, was the one-legged WWII PT boat skipper. In the very first episode, Captain Storm notices that his new crew will refer to him as "sir" or as "captain" but not as "skipper." Skipper is term of respect and affection; it's not a title. A commanding officer must prove himself before his crew will refer to him as skipper.

Commander Larry Smith was my skipper. He was a *hard-charging, damn the torpedoes, accomplish the mission, take care of the crew* warrior. He had a lot of pull and connections. Rumor was that he could have taken command of any warship in the fleet but that he wanted the *USS McKean (DD-784)*. He could have been the CO of a brand new, state of the art, *Spruance*-class DD, but because the *McKean* was homeported in Seattle, he selected that thirty-plus year old veteran of World War Two. I'm grateful that he made that choice.

He worked us hard. We spent days on end practicing NGFS — naval gunfire support — blasting away at any target he could get us. "The ship is called a destroyer, so damn it, we're going to *destroy* something." We would practice GQ drills over and over and over until we got it right and *exceeded* his standards. Every sailor on board knew his job, knew what was expected of him and damn well better have known a few other jobs too. If Captain Smith wanted us to win the COMCRUDESGRU 5's ASW award, we better have some practice blowing up submarines. He had enough clout to obtain ASROC weapons when there weren't supposed to be any available and he could arrange for us to have a real submarine to shoot at. On one visit to San Diego, another destroyer was moored at Quay Wall #1. That was a very desirable spot due its close proximity to the EM club. He determined that the CO of that destroyer was junior to him so he had it moved and we moored in its spot.

We spent a great deal of time in SoCal (Southern California) waters. The area offered training and repair facilities we just couldn't get back home. In February 1978, we were in San Diego for a CSRT (Combat Systems Readiness Test — a very thorough going over of all the ship's weapons systems) and REFTRA (Refresher Training, a grueling week-long simulated battle problem).

On 20 February, I returned to the ship after a weekend leave. It was after lights out and I kept trying to work the combination on my locker. I couldn't get it to open. I finally realized that it wasn't my lock that was on my locker. "WTF?" I was baffled at first. And then I developed a theory. We were expecting a new 1st-class sonar tech onboard soon. Why, that SOB must have reported onboard while I was on leave and he pulled rank and bounced me out of my locker. The more I thought about it, the more sense it made and the madder I got. The only appropriate thing I could think of doing, the perfect solution to this dilemma was for me to get even more pissed, summon all of my strength and then punch out my metal locker.

The locker won. I instantly knew that I had made a very unwise decision. The punch made a hell of a racket but my jumping up and down like an organ-grinder's monkey and my screaming, "@#&$$*%(#), that hurts!!," woke up TM3 Mike Ring. Mike said, "Hey, welcome back. Right after you left, they couldn't find the AS-ROC magazine keys. They checked the log and you were the last one to sign out for them. So the day you left, the Master at Arms and the ASW officer cut the lock on your locker, found the ASROC keys and put a new lock on your locker for you." Mike handed me a piece of paper and added, "Here's the combination. Sure is good to have you back. Good night."

I should have felt really stupid but my left hand hurt too much. I crawled, carefully, into my third-level high rack and went to sleep.

Reveille was sounded about five hours later. I tried to hop out of my rack but my hand was now throbbing. I couldn't grab hold of the chain that supported my rack and crawl out, as I usually did. I had to devise a new technique to get down. I knew something was seriously wrong. The Navy legend of the sailor who caught a nasty sunburn and was written up for destruction of government property came to mind and I realized that I needed a cover story to explain how I hurt my hand. At Sick Call, I explained to HMC Gruell that as I was coming onboard late at night, I accidentally closed a weatherdeck hatch while my hand was still on the knife-edge. He seemed to buy the story and suggested that I soak the hand in cold water.

The next day, my hand hurt even worse and Doc Gruell handed me some aspirin and told me to continue to soak the hand in cold water. The third day I got more aspirin and was told to switch to warm water. On day four, I got an ace bandage. I toughed it out for six more days but finally couldn't stand it anymore. Doc Gruell implied that I was being a wimp but he cut me a chit to go to the base dispensary where they could take a look at it.

The base's corpsmen x-rayed my hand and it plainly showed three broken bones. They put me on a fleet taxi and I was sent to Balboa Naval Hospital. The Navy doctors there saw that since it had been ten days since the unfortunate "accident with that hatch" and the break was already starting to heal, but healing incorrectly. Without warning, the doctor twisted my hand and re-broke all three fractures. He x-rayed me again and put a cast on my hand. I caught the next fleet taxi back to the base. As the taxi made its rounds, I got off at the Exchange to do some shopping.

So as not to be confused with all of the other bases in the San Diego area, Naval Station San Diego is more commonly called, "32nd Street." The base is on one side of 32nd Street and the Exchange, the Petty Officer's club and the CPO club are on the other. Naval regulations prohibited sailors from wearing dungarees off base unless on official duty. The only exception was the exchange. To go to the exchange, one could walk out the main gate in dungarees to go but you could *not* drive out in a civilian car. Since I wore my dungarees to Balboa, I could *walk* back through the main gate onto the base and still be legal.

I purchased the items I thought a partial-cripple like me would need to survive on: the current editions of *Hot Rod* and *Playboy* magazines, two cans of snuff, shaving cream and a Tanya Tucker cassette. My last stop before leaving the exchange was the Baskins & Robbins ice cream parlor. At the front of the line was my skipper, Commander Larry Smith. We exchanged greetings and he asked about my hand. I gave him the short version, broke on a hatch, x-ray at dispensary, cast at Balboa and fleet taxi ride to here. I omitted that part of Doc Gruell's less-than-thorough diagnosis. I learned a long time ago never to piss of the PNs (they write your orders), DKs (they pay you), SHs (they cut your hair and do your laundry), MSs (they feed you) and HMs (they stick needles in your arm or strange objects up your wazoo — and they can also toss your shot record over the side).

Captain Smith said that he had his rental car parked outside and he offered me a ride back to the ship. I couldn't say no. So with him in his khakis and me in my dungarees, we got into his Ford Fairmont and drove across 32nd Street straight for the main gate. *(Okay, can you see where this story is going now? I've set the stage, I've in-*

troduced the characters, I've explained the background and now I can see your anxiety is building. Let's go straight to the conflict and the essence of this sea story.)

Manning the gate at Naval Station San Diego are honest to goodness United States Marines. No rent-a-cops at this fleet facility. As we approached the gate, Captain Smith and I both displayed our military ID cards. Instead of waving us through as they did almost all of the time, the PFC motioned for Captain Smith to halt. He saluted and asked, very politely, "May I examine your IDs please, sir?" He was handed both of our ID cards. He then asked, again very politely, "Sir, are you familiar with the rules regarding the wearing of dungarees while driving through this gate while wearing dungarees?"

Captain Smith replied, "Private, I'm not wearing dungarees." The PFC then said, "I realize that, Sir. I was referring to your passenger." (i.e., Me.)

Captain Smith was starting to get a little annoyed. Still seated in his Ford, he adjusted his posture so that the scrambled eggs on his combination cap were right at the marine's eye level. "Private," he said, "this is my petty officer. He broke his hand on my ship. I am returning him to my ship."

Well, I thought. That should resolve this matter.

Without missing a beat, the Marine gate guard said, "Yes Sir. However, it is against the rules for an enlisted man to wear dungarees while in a car crossing this gate."

I was about to suggest that I just get out and walk when Captain Smith said, "Private, this is MY Petty Officer. He broke his hand on MY ship while carrying out MY orders!" *I did?* "I drove him to Balboa hospital where they put a cast on his hand and now I am driving him back to MY ship!" For emphasis, Captain Smith grabbed my left wrist and yanked it towards the Marine so that he could plainly see the cast. It hurt like hell when he did that but I didn't think that was the time to say anything.

The PFC stepped back like he thought Captain Smith was going to strike him with my cast. He regained his composure and said, "Yes Sir. Do you have any paperwork indicating that is what happened?"

Holy shit! I thought. This guy is dedicated but he's not too bright.

"PRIVATE," Captain Smith said very loud and very slowly, "I'm telling you that's what happened."

Just to prove my opinion of him correct, the PFC said, "I understand that, Sir, but I need to see some paperwork indicating that that is what happened."

Oh, he shouldn't have said that. It's going to get really ugly.

"PRIVATE, I am a full $&%(*^+ Commander and the $&% (*^+ Commanding Officer of the $&%(*^+ *USS McKean* and I am $&%(*^+ telling you that is what happened and if you want to see any $&%(*^+ paperwork you can get your $&%(*^+ ass down to $&%(*^+ Quay Wall One (*he really did like to moor there)* and I will have you escorted up to my $&%(*^+ stateroom where I will show you all the $&%(*^+ paperwork you are ever going to want to $&% (*^+ see!"

Oh, $&%(, this isn't going well.

"Yes Sir. Perhaps if you were to drive over to the OOD shack and explain it to the OOD, he might issue a pass."

Oh, $&%(.

"I'll $&%(*^+ just do that PRIVATE and you better be there too."

"I'm sorry Sir but I'm on duty and I cannot leave my post."

"WELL THEN GET YOUR $&%(*^+ ASS RELIEVED!!!"

With that, Captain Smith dropped it into gear and left skid marks straight for the OOD shack. I turned around and could see our gate guard inside his shack frantically trying to dial *anybody* on his telephone. Captain Smith screeched to a stop in front of the OOD shack and said to me, "Hood, stay in the car." I did what that Marine should have done. I said, "Aye, aye, sir."

Now I couldn't hear what was said inside the OOD office, but from where the car was parked I could see into the office perfectly. I could tell quite plainly what was being said inside. Let me describe it. Captain Smith stepped inside. The first person inside was a Marine second lieutenant, who was seated at a desk busy writing something. He barely glanced at Captain Smith and, concentrating at his work, asked, "Can I help you?"

Captain Smith yelled out, "Yes. You can get on your $&% (*^+ feet when addressing a superior officer!"

Oh, this just got worse. Somehow, this is all going to be my fault.

The second louie popped tall and shouted, "Sir. Sorry Sir." And then Captain Smith unloaded on him. "What kind of $*%&%# Mickey Mouse, insubordinate, #U$&$^$, outfit are you running here? Don't you teach your (#$*%& gate guards to #@)_$&% any $&%(*^+ smarts? What the $&%(is wrong with you people anyway?"

That was a really poor moment for our PFC to walk into the OOD shack. Captain Smith started thumping the PFC in the chest with his finger and then started thumping the second louie in the chest also. He didn't skip a beat going on about "*%#+@!~(~"{<!!." He made so much noise that someone in an interior office opened a door to see just what all the commotion was about. It was an honest-to-goodness Admiral.

I'm screwed.

The admiral had this 'WTF?' look on his face. He first saw the two terrified Marines standing at attention, sweat pouring down their faces. I was worried that he would activate a secret panic-button that would summon the entire base security force. Instead, he looked over towards the source of this turmoil and stared straight at my skipper.

"Larry!" the admiral exclaimed.

"Bob!"

Bob? He called an Admiral, 'Bob?'

"I didn't know you were in San Diego?"

"Pulled in two weeks ago."

"You didn't call. Janet would love to have you over for dinner."

"I've been meaning to but I wanted to get CSRT & REFTRE over with first."

"Ah, that will keep you busy. Let's have lunch ASAP. Now, Larry, what the hell is all of this about?"

"Glad you asked. This $#)$?%>.{#_#$)%)#_ paperwork (#*$&%^#$,.{}+)# broken hand)#)#)_+2` _#(dungarees)$+%+% $+%(%&@/"].!"

"He did?"

"And then when I came in here, this #($_${:"@(#6$_)>sitting at his desk!"

"He didn't!"

And then like that scene in the movie *Patton* where George C. Scott whacks the shell-shocked soldier, the admiral started thumping his finger on the chest of the second lieutenant and cursing even worse then my skipper had been.

I'm going to make it through this okay.

With that, the admiral and my captain shook hands, exchanged phone numbers and Captain Smith drove me straight back to the ship. He didn't say a word. I spent the rest of the work day hiding in the ASROC weapons magazine where no one could have found me.

For the next few days, the officers on the ship looked at me kind of funny but they didn't say anything either. Every time I walked through the 32nd Street gate, I kept looking for that same PFC but I never saw him again. Iran was heating up then. They probably needed dedicated marines at our embassy in Tehran.

Footnote: OPNAVINST 3120.32 sec 510.47 "No person shall use profane, obscene or vulgar words or gestures onboard a naval unit."

MONIKERS AND MORE

BY GARY WHITE

Almost everyone had one, both enlisted and officers. Some were obvious, "Boats," "Doc" and "Cookie." Some you had to think about or know the person to whom it was attached. A few of the more memorable ones from my shipboard days were "Magilla Gorilla," "C.W. Moss," "Teddy Bear" and "High Pockets." All were used in the day-to-day camaraderie between shipmates and most weren't meant to be harmful, only descriptive.

"Magilla Gorilla" was a seaman apprentice when I reported aboard my first ship. Assigned to WG Division, he gave the appearance of a classic *deck ape*, hard working, hard drinking and rough around the edges. Until you really got to know him, you wouldn't give him much thought. But "Magilla" was a sleeper. The nickname, that of a popular 1960s cartoon character, came from both his size and demeanor. Prior to the start of his service in the Navy, he had worked much of his life in the logging camps of Oregon and his physical appearance proved it. At 5'10" and 195 pounds he was a mass of pure muscle. Biceps measured almost 17 inches around and he gave the impression of a concrete block with legs. If he hit you on the arm in the every day horseplay among friends, you never forgot it.

We once watched him hoist four five gallon cans of paint from the *yingyang* hole, a storage area located five decks below the main deck in the bow, hand over hand using only his strength and a rope. Not all that impressive unless you happened to be there. Standing on top of the cans, holding onto the rope was a 5'6" gunner's mate who weighted in at about 120 lb. When the load reached the main deck, "Magilla" reached down with one hand and lifted the gunner's mate out of the hole while holding the rope with the other. Then the paint cans emerged.

So now you're probably thinking "Okay, so he's an incredibly strong deck ape, but still a deck ape." Well, yes and no. While he was never destined to be a rocket scientist, he had the practical nature and sense of humor that made him a friend to everyone aboard, officers and enlisted alike. If you asked him a question, you got a straight and honest answer. If you needed a friend to cover your backside in a tense situation, he was always nearby. While calculus might have been beyond his capability, he did some of the best *busy work* railings I ever saw. When I departed the ship fifteen months later, "Magilla" had made Boatswain's Mate 3rd class and was the most dependable and dedicated member of the deck division.

"C.W. Moss" earned his moniker the moment he crossed the gangway to report for duty in 1968. He could have been a twin brother to Michael J. Pollard, the Oscar- nominated actor who played the service station attendant turned bank robbing accomplice C.W. Moss in the 1967 movie *Bonnie & Clyde*. Our version looked, walked and talked just like the original and if she didn't know better, would have fooled even Pollard's mother. He was amicable and good natured about his nickname and even used it on occasion to procure a free drink or two in a couple of ports that the ship visited. A seaman in the supply division, "C.W." was working on a yeoman rating when I departed the ship.

"Teddy Bear" was exactly what he was called, a teddy bear. That's how he was introduced to me when I reported to my second duty station and it fit him to a 'T' the entire time I knew him. Mellow, and always smiling, I don't think I ever saw him angry in the few months I was aboard. Patience is something that quite a few young sailors lack but that was "Teddy Bear's" character and it showed in everything he did or was responsible for in our division. From the Pacific Northwest, he and I, along with one other shipmate departed the ship at the same time heading for separation and a return to civilian life. As luck would have it, we ended up closing our Navy careers in his hometown. He stayed there, and we hopped on a plane one cold and rainy day in January, 1970.

"High Pockets" was a tall lanky officer aboard one of my duty ships. He earned the nickname because of his height and high waist-line. A highly intelligent lieutenant (j.g.), he was assigned a critical billet aboard the ship. So it was a surprise when the enlisted cadre aboard learned that in the wee hours of the morning while on station in the Gulf of Tonkin, he did one of the dumbest things he could have in furthering his career. At about 2:20 am, the ship was called to general quarters, based on a suspicious surface contact on a heading toward the ship. "High Pockets," asleep in his cabin in Officers Country, awoke at the sound of GQ and promptly telephoned the bridge to inquire whether or not the call to General Quarters was a drill. Unfortunately for him, the captain was already on the bridge and was handed the phone. The enlisted contingent heard about the response of the captain from those on the bridge at the time. Suffice it to say that "High Pockets" was at his assigned GQ station in record time after that.

Monikers, nicknames, or whatever noun you prefer, they were always present and interesting. You may not remember the real names of the people they attached to but it rarely matters. To those who knew them they will always be "Magilla," "C.W.," "Teddy Bear," "High Pockets," or whatever moniker they earned from their friends.

THE ADVENTURES OF SEAMAN CINDY

BY DICK KING

On July 14, 1967, the *USS Chevalier (DD-805)* pulled into Victoria, British Columbia, as part of a five ship American delegation to help celebrate the Canadian Naval Centennial, and simultaneously, the British Columbia Centennial. We were greeted warmly upon our arrival, with almost as much enthusiasm as when we finally departed, about a week later. But that's another story. Sometime during our tumultuous fun-filled stay, one or more of the boatswain's mates smuggled a small puppy on board and hid her in the boatswain's locker.

By the time we were almost back to San Diego, the only person on board unaware of the stowaway was the captain, G. G. Ely Kirk. The XO finally gave the boatswain's mates an ultimatum: tell the captain. A small delegation of boatswain's mates approached the captain on the bridge, confessed what they had done and asked him for permission to keep the puppy on board as the ship's mascot. The captain sat there for a minute and then said, "Well, how can I make a decision until I have seen the dog?" Smiles broke out everywhere.

The puppy was rushed to the bridge, and apparently she passed inspection because she was enlisted on the spot for a one-year tour, including the 1967/68 deployment. The dog was named "Cindy" (which coincidentally was the name of the captain's teen-aged daughter), given the rank of Seaman Apprentice and assigned to First Division.

SA Cindy adjusted bit by bit to life on a destroyer and became a very popular shipmate. For most sailors, billets on the *Watch, Quarter and Station Bill* were handed down from on high. But for Cindy, she sort of found her own. Take for example her general quarters station. Part of the training workup for a WestPac deployment was gunnery drills. On the day of the first gunnery exercise after Cindy came on board, she was frolicking around the main deck. General Quarters was sounded, everyone rushed to their GQ Station, Condition Zebra was set (all doors and hatches shut tight) and in the process, Cindy was just plain overlooked and left out on deck.

Mount 51, on the fo'c'sle, was the first mount to fire, and when the pair of 5-inch guns went off, SA Cindy was directly under the gun barrels. She bounced about three feet in the air, and then took off running aft. She arrived on the fantail under Mount 53 just as it too fired. Her plight, however, had been observed by the bridge watch and the lookouts and orders were given to break Condition Zebra and let her into the deckhouse. She proceeded immediately to Damage Control Central (Engineering Log Room), almost exactly in between the forward and after gun mounts, and curled up at the feet of the phone talkers. From that day forward, whenever GQ was sounded, Cindy would race on her own, to Damage Control Central and remain there patiently until Secure from GQ was sounded.

As time went on, Cindy found her place on other watch bills. For the Special Sea and Anchor Detail, entering or leaving port, she stood Forward Lookout, with her nose sticking out through the bull nose (the ring at the very tip of the bow through which a tow rope or mooring hawser could be passed). In port, she spent most of her waking hours standing quarterdeck watch at the brow. Seaman Cindy (she had by now been promoted) never mastered ladders, so she stood watch, ate, slept and hung out on the main deck, both inboard and outboard. By the time the *Chevalier* arrived in Olongopo, Philippines,

Seaman Cindy knew every member of the crew, about 270 total, and would vigorously challenge any non-crewmember coming up the *Chevalier's* brow.

During our short first stay in Olongopo, the Subic Bay SRF (Ship Repair Facility) was doing an emergency overnight job in the forward fireroom replacing the number one boiler main steam outlet elbow. It was a critical and important job because that boiler constituted a quarter of our propulsion capability and we were supposed to leave in the morning for Vietnam. While enjoying a few gin and tonics at the *O* club on base, knowing they would be the last gin and tonics I would have for a long time, I received a phone call from the duty engineer. I was told that the Ship Repair Facility *yard birds* (civilian workers) working on the boiler had gone on strike and were sitting on the pier. They refused to go back to work until we got rid of "that vicious guard dog." I rushed back to the ship and locked Cindy up in the air-conditioned electronics workshop. After some persuasion and assurances, the Filipino workers went back to work and the *Chevalier* got underway in the morning, with the last of the workers having to climb over the rail to the pier because the brow had already been removed.

Sometime in October of 1967, while the *Chevalier* was engaged in naval gunfire support for Army and Marine units ashore in Vietnam, Seaman Cindy hurt her leg. She was put on the *binnacle list* (too sick or injured to carry out her duties). A few days later, when the Chevy steamed into Kaosiung, Taiwan for a tender availability period, there was an arrival conference in the wardroom. Work requests were reviewed and approved or rejected. At some point during the conference, the captain of the tender remarked that he had excellent medical and dental facilities. Captain Kirk replied that he had "one sailor needing attention," but didn't explain it any further.

Thirty minutes after the conference concluded, however, Seaman Cindy was in the tender's sickbay, much to the surprise of the doctor and corpsmen. The doctor took an x-ray and concluded that Cindy had a broken leg. The fracture was set and a plaster cast with an aluminum tip was applied. The story of Seaman Cindy's treatment was put into the tender's Plan of the Day as a news item, and before the TAV was cut short by an approaching typhoon, the tender delivered to the Chevy a beautiful wood dog bed, stained, varnished and upholstered, with suction cups on the bottom to grip the deck in heavy weather and an engraved nameplate on the side. The bed was placed in the aft athwartships passageway opposite the ship's store.

Cindy took to it without hesitation, obviously liked it and in time re-covered completely.

The amazing thing about the tender's gift was that no Work Request (Form OPNAV 4700-2C) was ever submitted in triplicate and approved in quadruplicate to "fabricate dog bed for medium sized dog." Cindy's bed was the only tender job I can remember which was completed without a duly prepared and signed OPNAV 4700-2C.

Captain Kirk, through his influence in high places, had man-aged to retain command of the *Chevalier* for almost three years, a year longer than the normal Bureau of Personnel pattern of rotation. At the very end of this deployment, we headed for Brisbane, Austra-lia. Just before departing for Brisbane, however, Captain Kirk's relief came on board. While the outgoing captain and the soon to be new captain went through the turnover process, we crossed the equator and had to go through the proper *crossing the line* ceremonies. In these ceremonies, *shell backs* (sailors who have crossed the equator before) initiate *polliwogs* (sailors crossing for the first time). Seaman Cindy, of course, was a polliwog and had to go through the same gauntlets as her lowly peers, including a crawl through *the garbage chute* and *kissing the belly of the Royal Baby*. At the end of the cere-monies, everyone was issued about three beers each. This was even more illegal than having a dog on board, and the soon-to-be new cap-tain just had to take it all in. Change of Command ceremonies were held while we were in Brisbane and Captain Kirk flew home to the states.

Upon returning to San Diego, I overheard the new captain, Commander Glen Palatini, tell the XO that although Seaman Cindy seemed to be a good sailor, very popular with the crew, the XO needed to start looking for a way to transfer her off the ship in a man-ner which would not hurt morale. A few weeks thereafter, while the Chevy was tied to pier six in San Diego, liberty call was sounded and everyone not in the duty section rushed down the brow at 32 knots, including the captain, the XO and all department heads.

I was the CDO and about a half hour later, I was just standing on the fantail exchanging scuttlebutt with other sailors who also had the duty. As usual, Seaman Cindy was hanging out in the same gen-eral area where she could keep an eye on the brow. Someone noticed a gray official Navy sedan coming down the pier, sporting a pennant on the fender with two stars on it, and called it to my attention. Since no official flag visit was expected, and since we were opposite the pier from a new DLG (guided missile destroyer leader, about twice the Chevy's size), I assumed the admiral's destination was the DLG.

The car stopped midway between the two ships; an aide jumped out, opened the rear door on the *Chevalier* side, and out bounced an admiral who then headed straight for our brow. Oh, shit! I risked the guess that this was our flotilla commander, although I had never met or even seen him, and told the watch to bong him aboard as such. Even as sweat was forming under my cover, by the time the admiral was halfway up the brow, I suddenly had a new problem. Seaman Cindy couldn't tell the difference between an admiral and a seaman recruit and in her mind, he was just an intruder! Accordingly, she went into her alarm mode and began barking louder than I had ever heard before.

As the somewhat startled admiral saluted the national ensign, I grabbed Cindy's collar with my left hand and a few seconds later rendered one of the most memorable salutes that admiral ever received, holding Cindy by her collar and therefore in a very crooked version of attention. Then the admiral asked, "Is this part of the ship's security program?"

My reply was "Yes Sir! She knows every member of the crew and she alerts the watch if a non-crewmember is coming aboard." Thankfully, Cindy had stopped barking and her tail was now wagging. The admiral bent over and petted Seaman Cindy while asking first if the captain was on board, and then if the XO was on board. After learning that neither were on board, the admiral said, "Tell the captain I dropped by," turned around and departed as quickly as he had arrived. In the morning, I duly reported the surprise flag visit, but left out the part concerning Cindy's greeting.

Seaman Cindy was the best friend of every member of the crew, but to her, some of her friends were better than others. At the very top of her list were the ship's cooks who prepared and served her meals just inside the galley door. Shortly after the admiral incident, the XO learned that one of the cooks was going to retire to a family farm in northern California. After a brief conference between the cook and the XO, it was quickly agreed that there would be a double retirement ceremony, much to the XO's relief.

When the big day came, there were the requisite six sideboys in full dress white and a boatswain's mate with his boatswain's pipe. Although it was a Saturday, a large crowd gathered on the fantail. The cook went down the brow first, to the traditional pipe and announcement. A moment later, the pipe was repeated: "Seaman Cindy,

United States Navy Retired, departing," was announced over the loudspeakers and Cindy was led down the brow to the car belonging to the cook's family! Her service in the United States Navy was thereby honorably completed and so far as was known, she lived happily ever after.

UNAUTHORIZED GEAR

BY TERRY MILLER

Just prior to a two-year WestPac deployment in June of 1968, the *USS George K. MacKenzie (DD-836)* underwent a substantial crew change. Gone was popular Executive Officer, Commander Van Antwerp, to his own command. The new XO was Lieutenant Commander Alvin Feingersch. Commander Feingersch made no attempt to follow the lead of his predecessor's popularity, but of course being liked by the crew is not really part of an XO's duties. If being disliked by the crew is a part of those duties then Feingersch did his job well. We usually dreaded his presence because of the changes his arrival made to our routine.

One of the first changes he made was to institute regular Friday field days and zone inspections. Okay, so maybe the ship was not as spic and span as it should have been and maybe getting us into a routine of cleanliness wasn't such a bad idea. It was change and sailors everywhere universally resist change. Especially if there is an increase in work involved.

It amazed me that the senior petty officers didn't find these new inspections nearly as offensive as I did. After all, it required that they watch us lowly E-3s and E-4s clean, move their feet occasionally lest a wet swab touch their shoes, and at times, even get up and move to a different chair. It was a hardship but they bore it well.

The XO was diligent in visiting every occupied compartment and workspace aboard the ship every Friday. I don't know how he managed to inspect them all personally but I have to give him credit for getting it done. I also have to give him credit for finding nearly all the places where we might have cut corners in cleaning. I doubt anyone passed that first Friday but he didn't hold that one against us. However, woe be unto the lowly seaman or fireman who stood by in white hat, ready with a snappy salute to present a less-than-spotless space the following week.

Sonar Control and UB Plot cleaning duties were shared between fellow sonarman, Barney Matthews and I, and being junior to Barney I got the privilege of making the presentation when the XO came by to inspect. Since he began his inspections at the Signal shack on the 03 level and worked his way down, we were among the first to be inspected. This was a mixed blessing. It meant that we had less time to clean the space than compartments lower in the ship but it also meant that we didn't have to stand around not getting it dirty all afternoon! Granted, not a lot of muddy or grease-laden boots came our way (fifteen feet or so of CIC lay between us and the nearest passageway which meant those same muddy boots had to get past both the CIC watch officer and Radarman Chief Kemp. Some of the officers assigned there might not look at a man's boots but no one was going to track dirt into CIC while the chief was around and he preferred to survey his domain from the chair by the door to Sonar. This also meant that any contraband scheduled for Sonar had to wait until the chief was away but that's a story for another time).

So the extent of the field day for me consisted of swabbing the rubber matting that lay on top of the removable deck plates, cleaning up around the coffee mess, emptying the butt kits, and taking out the trash. It also included rolling up the aforementioned rubber mat and lifting out one of the removable deck plates to expose the crawl space for wire runs underneath. While the deck plate was open, any and all contraband was stashed there, the plate returned, and the rubber mat rolled flat again. Barney's twelve-string guitar wouldn't fit under the deck plates but there was space inside one of the three large fire control computer cabinets for at least a half dozen guitars had we had them, so hiding one was never a problem.

After that initial visit, the XO spent about 60 seconds in my space and while he was not one to tell us we had done a good job, he didn't ding us on anything, either. Barney and I had a reciprocal and equitable agreement. As senior E-3, he would share any honors for a clean space. As junior E-3, I did not have to share any of the blame with him. I could keep it all.

Four decks down in the Sonar Equipment Room just off the WA Division berthing compartment forward of and one deck below the mess decks, another sonarman stood waiting for the XO's inspection. We had a phone between the two spaces so we could call down and tell Terry "Mort" Mortensen what kind of mood Feingersch was in and what time he had left us so they could gauge his arrival at their level. They had a lot more contraband to stow down there than we had. Everyone used the equipment room as a Sonar Lounge, it being right off the berthing compartment. I kept my own guitar there and a small record collection, someone else had a reel-to-reel tape recorder there, another had a stereo with a community turntable. Also in the space was a small boxy, white refrigerator perched on top of a large, boxy gray equipment cabinet. On the bulkheads were fifteen or twenty pinups and centerfold pictures from various men's magazines. I mean, the guys bought those magazines for the articles, you understand, and they had to do something with the photos besides letting them clutter up the pages of the fine articles in *Playboy* and *Penthouse*, didn't they? Of course. Well, the XO had himself a field day and phrases like, "unauthorized gear" and "smutty pictures" were most of what he had to say that first Friday in the Sonar Equipment Room.

Apparently he did not appreciate art so down came the photos and most of the unauthorized gear found space in cabinets and inside little-used large, gray, boxy equipment. Mort, Mike, Ben, Randy, and Lennie decided to leave the refrigerator and base its presence there on the argument that there was a refrigerator in the Boatswain's locker where the BMs sold cold soft drinks at certain times of the day. We're just doing what they are doing, was to be the proposed argument.

The following Friday, after I called down to let them know that the XO had finished his minute in Sonar Control, the group gathered in the equipment room to lend moral support to Mort's attempt the get the XO to let us keep the fridge.

"Unauthorized gear. I don't want to see this refrigerator next time I inspect. I just told the Boatswain's Mates the same thing. Not authorized. Get it out of here."

So much for our argument. A high-level meeting of the senior petty officers came up with the solution. They removed the fridge's handle and painted the outside of it with the same machinery gray as every other gray box in the space and moved it to the top of another equipment cabinet in another part of the compartment. For the rest of the time he was aboard, the XO walked right past it each week without so much as a glance at its shiny gray finish. Those cold Cokes tasted even better than they had before.

I HAVE THE MISSILE KEYS

BY KEN DANDURAND

The Damage Control Central watch on this fine new DLGN, the *USS South Carolina (DLGN-37)* was a boring watch for the most part. One passed the time by reading, talking to the snipes on the 21MC, talking to the roving patrols, or trying to get someone to bring down something from the galley like fresh pastries, which could be smelled through the air supply vents.

Another pastime was trying to emulate MR1 Dougherty's penmanship. He was from Scotland and his writing was to die for. Everyone that stood watches tried to copy his style while making log entries. The best description I can make of the writing style was free-hand calligraphy.

As the Officer Corps of the Navy are so oft to point out,"idle hands are the Devil's workshop." While on the 1200-1600 watch one day I noticed how lax the officers were when it came to security protocol and the missile keys they were charged with. The keys, one assigned to the Weps Officer and one to the Ops Officer, were kept in small wall mount safes in Damage Control Central. These are the same safes that most every officers' stateroom had by their desks to store security papers and candy bars. They are opened with a combination, then the keys are retrieved, the missile house is unlocked and the Harpoon missiles and ASROC are made ready for firing.

I noticed that when retrieving the keys, the officers never shielded the combinations with their bodies. I could sit at my desk and look at a 45-degree angle to my left and see the combination dials quite clearly. So, as a challenge to myself, I watched the next time they removed the keys. I found that I obtained the first two numbers from the Weps safe the first time. I made mental note. When they returned the keys I got the final number. Easy as pie. The next time they came to get the keys I got one number of the Ops safe and then got the second number when they returned the keys. I tried the next several times to get the last number, but since the safe was on the right of the other one it was more of an angle for me to see. The normal placement of the body while opening the safe was obscuring my view.

Another natural place for the Damage Control Central Watch

to be was at the end of the room looking at the charts and info sheets. This put me at about 30 degrees from the safe and about six feet away. To get the last number I merely looked at the charts until I perceived it was time to dial in the last number and I turned around and *voila!* He was on 14. I turned back around and that was that.

Later that night, while on watch, I had to test my theory. I thought, "They may have changed a combination since it has been four days since I started this. Well, let's try it!" I mean after all, I passed my own criteria for FTS (Final Top Secret). So after all the people had left, I walked over to the Weps safe and entered the combination, turned the handle and opened the door. I quickly closed it and spun the combination. I went over and sat down at the desk again and thought, "Whew, one down!" I sat there for a few minutes and then went over to the Ops safe and spun the dial, then turned the handle and opened the door. I again quickly closed the door and spun the combination. Quite satisfied with myself and feeling a little giddy with my newfound "power status" I returned to my desk.

I thought about this for a while…you know, like the rest of the watch. How easy would it be for someone else to do what I had done? Would they be as honest, albeit conniving, as me? What should I do? It became obvious to me that something should be done on my part and silence was out of the question. I thought, okay, whom do I tell? The CO? Nah. The XO? Maybe. The Weps and Ops Officers? Nah. My DCA? Nah…he may not pass my Security standards. Who do I feel most comfortable with this information? Who could rectify it immediately without getting the two officers and me both in trouble?

I had become quite close to the first CO, Captain Kneel, but he was gone and the new CO, Captain Simonton, was a real Navy man. Everything was by the book. Although I knew he liked and trusted me, Nah! The only logical choice (in my mind) was the XO, Commander Hickson.

I still hesitated because security is a serious (if not stupid) thing in the service. People are given guns and told they can use deadly force and their only screening was that they scored high on their GCT-ARIs, so they were sent to "Missileer" school instead of the knuckledragging "Paint-Chipping-U." I sure didn't want to go to prison or get in hot water, so I decided to play it one step at a time.

What would have made the entire process safer? Maybe putting a shield around the combination wheel so it could only be viewed from straight on. God, I'm good, I thought. I can ID a problem and come up with the answer to it. Now, how do I implement it? I can't just start welding a piece of bent metal to the safe. First of all everyone would have a hemorrhage. Second, the close proximity of the weld would melt the plastic mechanism of the combination and make the safe useless. Could I just tell the DCA? Nope. He would probably say "Don't worry about it. The keys are safe."

I saw the XO in the second deck passageway and saluted him while saying "Good morning XO." He asked me how I was (this is a trick question he picked up from the CO. It doesn't mean how are you; it means give me a brief status report, if there is anything outside of normal). I always thought this was a way of learning something so they could trick their department heads and JOs during lunch chatter, i.e. "Well, Mr. Sadd, how are things in your department?"

"Fine Sir."

"How about in your Division, Mr. Sack?"

"Fine, Sir."

"Well, what about the P-250 that was dropped down the ladder in aft berthing and broken? Does that or the theft of the tool box from the shipfitter shop sound fine?" Nice little conversations like this are what I envisioned.

I continued on because I had stopped and thus he had stopped, making him eligible for further conversation. We enlisted learn these little nuances that allow us to circumvent Chain of Command. I said to him, "XO, when I am standing watch in DCC, I see things that bother me."

He responded "Like what?"

So I continue: "Security is supposed to be a paramount concern for us watchstanders and that is why the keys to the missiles are kept down there, we are manned 24 hours a day. The problem that I see is that anyone could get the combinations to the safes and obtain the keys."

"No, Dandurand, they are very careful not to let anyone see the combination."

"Well Sir, (I hesitated) that is not really correct," I answered.

The XO said, "What do you mean?"

I answered "If someone wanted, they could see the combination just by watching them open the safes from the sides of where they are standing."

He said, "No, they cover themselves when opening them."

"Not always" was my reply. I could tell he was challenging me now. "I can sit in my chair and see the combinations and then I would have them."

"Let's go see," he said.

So we walked down to DCC and I told the watch to stand up for a while. I asked the XO to sit in my chair, and he did. Then I went over to the safe and said, "This is where they stand to open the safes. See, you can see the numbers from there." He said nothing. I stepped to the other safe and said, "See, you can see the numbers from there." He said nothing.

He looked at the safes for a while and then said, "Well Dandurand, I understand what you are saying, but I don't think anyone could get the combination, and they would need the combination to both safes."

"Oh, it could be done sir … believe me!" I said as I looked straight in his eyes. He looked right back at me and knew what I was alluding to. "Do you know the combination to the safe (singular)," he asked.

"No Sir," I replied. "I know the combination to *both* safes."

UH-OHHH! Security breach!

"Let's see."

He had me relieve the watch and told the sailor to leave. He then called the CO and the two department heads (Weps and Ops). The CO did not come down, but the two department heads did. The XO told them what we had talked about and turned to me and asked, "Have you ever taken the keys out?" To which I answered, "No sir! I have never touched them."

"Okay, Dandurand, let's see you open the safes," the XO directed. I walked over to each one, entered the combination, and opened the doors. I could not see their expressions, but God how I wish I could have.

So it was silent for a while. The XO looked at the Weps and Ops bosses and said, "You know the drill." I sat at my desk facing away from the safes and I am quite sure the XO watched me also. The key holders verified that the proper keys were in the safes and changed the combinations.

The XO asked how long before I could have the pieces made and installed and I told him one hour. I called down to the shop and told my guys what I wanted made and they made the two C-shaped pieces that would cover the dials and I personally welded them on after the combination mechanisms were removed. The keys were reinserted, the combinations were changed and that was the last I ever heard of the situation.

COLD WARRIORS

BY BOB COHEN

My roommate, Danny Johns, had a very stressful job. He was the ship's Communications Officer. He spent most of his time in the air-conditioned radio shack, worrying about the security surrounding all the top-secret codes and other sensitive things that he was responsible for. He only had this job, he explained, because the last communications officer got bounced for some oversight he was accused of. Danny was sure that he himself was a prime candidate for a free trip to Leavenworth, but he was my friend and I tried my best to cheer him up. I pointed out to him that it could be worse — he could have to work in 110-degree heat in the fireroom like I did. He assured me that he'd work up quite a sweat breaking big rocks into smaller ones. I never did understand his free-floating anxiety, nor that of anyone else in the operations department. Then again, in engineering, we didn't have too many highly-classified things to burn you — just hot ones.

The radio shack had some kind of electric combination lock on the door. You couldn't open it unless you punched in a top-secret combination which was closely guarded and changed frequently in case we were infiltrated by enemy spies. I was taking a break in there one day, talking with Danny. Even though I wasn't near any of the gear that was hidden behind what resembled a canvas shower curtain (which ran from the deck all the way up to the overhead) it was probably a security violation for me to be there at all, but Danny was there with me... and after all, it was pretty much the coolest place on board. Something about the electronics, I guess.

Danny was behind the curtain fooling around with some gadget when I heard the barely noticeable sound of the combo lock getting punched. The door swings open, and the Ops boss walks in. He stops in sudden shock, seeing me sitting there all sweaty and oil-stained in the top-secret radio shack — and apparently alone. He stood there for a second with his mouth hanging open and his eyes blinking comically. "How did you get in here?" he whispered in a panic. I couldn't resist: "I don't know. I just kept pushing the buttons until the door opened. Lucky guess, huh?" Danny came out after he heard the thump.

Personally, I don't think people who are prone to fainting should be assigned to high-security work.

THE CAPTAIN'S GIG

BY MIKE SNYDER

While in Guantanamo Bay for refresher training in 1976, the CO of the *USS Claude V. Ricketts (DDG-5)* decided the department heads needed a break. On a Sunday, late in the training period, he called for his boat. The 1MC growled, "Away the gig, away," the traditional call to bring the captain's boat alongside. The CO, XO and four department heads piled into the gig accompanied by several cases of beer and a packed lunch for all. There was a coxswain and an engineer aboard to run the boat. It was sunny, bright, and hot. What else, on the south coast of Cuba?

We toured up into the upper reaches of Guantanamo Bay, found a pleasant spot, anchored, and went swimming. The water was warm and cloudy, but not dirty. We could see past the US Marine guard posts up toward Guantanamo City where Soviet ships were anchored. One passed us inbound through the bay under control of a Cuban pilot. Cuba had free access to the bay and the Soviets used it frequently to bring in material and haul out fruit.

Ships' boats of the US Navy are ugly, ungainly, and slow, and the *Ricketts* gig was no exception. As a deck officer and seaman I was always embarrassed when in company with ships of the European navies. They operated good-looking boats with great speed. Our gig was the standard fiberglass pig with a forward cockpit, a big, lumbering diesel engine well aft and an unattractive bulbous cover over the passenger compartment. We kept it painted and polished, but there was no getting around the design. The heavy engine aft made it squat in the water and its displacement and bluff bow combined to develop a big bow wave, looking to all the world like a tug. The Chief Engineer even tried changing the propeller in an effort to get it to plane to no avail. This Sunday, the weight of eight men aboard only forced her deeper into the water.

We had a pleasant few hours in the sun away from the ship. The beer was cold and the fried chicken tasty, especially when flavored with the sea salt still wet on your lips from the last plunge. As the sun began to fall into the west, we weighed anchor and, with engine racing, plodded down the bay toward our ship. Immediately we were surrounded by as many as ten bottlenosed dolphins. What a delight! I took a place all the way forward, on my belly, looking over the starboard side. The animals raced in and took station. Riding the big bow wave, absorbing the energy from the water with their tails, they flowed effortlessly alongside the boat. I was so close I was splashed when they beat with their tails. With my arm stretched over the side, fingers extended, I was continually within inches of touching the nearest surfer, but they never let me touch them. They breathed in with a quick sucking sound and left a trail of bubbles as they exhaled. Occasionally, one would roll onto its side and look directly into my eyes. I felt an immediate affinity for them. I would have liked to have gone into the water to be among them.

The dolphins vied for the best place in the wave and streaked away as each, in turn, was bumped or finessed out of position. They changed direction instantaneously, rolling and playing under and around the boat. Their clicks and whistles were clearly audible to everyone in the gig. We traveled this way for the better part of one half hour until they vanished, racing off at right angles to our course. They probably got bored with our slow advance. It was a remarkable encounter, one I thoroughly enjoyed and will never forget.

When lifted aboard the "*Claude V*" the gig lay in a gravity davit aft on the starboard side. During gun fire exercises the aft 5-inch gun sometimes fired forward of the starboard beam. When it did, the muzzle blast blew all the windows out of the gig, throwing them onto the deck in the enclosed compartment. Even though it was "my" boat for maintenance, I always took some delight in inflicting that little bit of torment on it. I hated that boat.

THE BATHYTHERMOGRAPH WINCH

BY TERRY MILLER

In case you've been lucky so far and didn't know that I was in the navy... Gotcha! I *was* in the navy. And like all good sailors, I know lots of sea stories. Some of them are even true. This is one of the true ones (you can tell because it doesn't start out with, "Now this is no bull!").

I was a sonar technician aboard the *USS George K MacKenzie (DD-836)*, a destroyer homeported in Yokosuka, Japan. Now the sonar rate was a good one to be in during Vietnam because an enemy submarine would find it difficult to hide in the relatively shallow waters of the Tonkin Gulf between Vietnam and China and the North Vietnamese Navy didn't have any submarines, anyway.

So what did we sonarmen do to earn our keep in this man's Navy? Well, we maintained an alert surveillance for Soviet or Chinese or other subs that might have been itching to start WWIII by attacking a WWII-vintage destroyer.

Of course, we maintained that surveillance in such places in the Western Pacific where such subs were not likely to be found. Didn't matter. We were ready for 'em. We kept our equipment in tiptop condition...except for the bathythermograph (that's from the Greek *bathys* for water, *thermo* for temperature, and *graph* for writing; darn those ancient Greeks, anyway). The bathythermograph, or BT, told us the temperature of the ocean at each depth so we'd know the thermal layers where a sub most likely would try to hide from us.

We had a new electronic BT model that allowed us to get readings every few hours just by releasing an inexpensive probe, but the old manual system was still welded to the deck on the fantail. It may even have worked; don't know. It just took up precious space that could have been used for something more productive, like sunbathing.

See, in the military, it doesn't matter whether a device works in the way it was designed. It only matters that no one wants to admit that something in their care doesn't work, even though the captain would have to be boiled in oil before he'd let us use the old thing. It required that the ship steer a straight line at slow speed for about 45 minutes while another thing that looked like a defective torpedo was lowered to a depth of a thousand feet or so and slowly brought back up. In other words, the ship was a sitting duck for the better part of an hour.

So, fellow sonar technicians Marty Martinez and Teddy Bear Mathis spent endless hours cleaning, greasing, and painting the thing and keeping it ready. You know, just in case. If, for example, the captain lost his mind and wanted to allow an enemy sub a really good shot at us. Oh, well, it kept those two guys out of trouble.

But word finally got out that it was never used. With deck space at a premium on a ship it wasn't long before three or four other groups started demanding the space, especially after we'd pulled into port alongside a sister ship that had already had her BT winch removed along with the boom that lowered the probe over the side of the ship and kept it out of her two 12-foot propellers.

"Hey," some sonarman from the *Henry W. Tucker* would say while we were tied up alongside her, "I see you still have that ancient BT winch. Didn't you know you could have it removed?" These guys had a way of letting the whole world find out that being a sonarman was an easy life. That wasn't quite the image we tried to project.

"How come you told us this was classified equipment?" they all wanted to know. "How come you keep all this space back here when the rest of us need it for real equipment? Let's hear what the captain has to say about this!" Oops! Now we had to put in a request to have the thing removed before the gunner's mates did.

"Uh, Cap'n, a sonarman over on the *Tucker* told us BuShips will now let us get rid of the BT winch. Do you want to check and see?" That was a lot like asking if your cat would be interested in a fresh can of tuna. The next time we were in port a swarm of yardbirds buzzed around the winch area for a couple of hours and it was gone.

Poor Marty. The big curved shield around the winch that kept the front of it out of sight was one of his favorite places to hide and sleep. He didn't plan to re-enlist anyway but certainly not if they were going to make us work.

SEABATS

BY MIKE SNYDER

USS Glover (AGDE-1), a research and development destroyer escort, routinely got underway with many civilian scientists and engineers aboard. I was never quite sure how they were selected, but suspected that in addition to being principals in the current batch of experiments and tests, Naval Underwater Systems Center (NUSC) New London had an informal program of sending young engineers to sea simply for the experience. Some of those boarding for a cruise were old hands that appeared over and over again, but many were new folks who might not have been aboard a ship before, and certainly never aboard the *Glover*.

Seabats invariably turn up during a quiet period within a few days of getting underway. The bridge would announce that a seabat had been captured and could be seen on the fantail. Grins went up all around and a small crowd casually gathered on the main deck and 01-level to watch the activities. Often sooner than later, in ones and twos, young, new sailors and first-time-at-sea engineers would drift aft to get a look at the seabat. Arriving aft they would find one of the crewmen down on his hands and knees looking at the bat through a hole in a medium sized cardboard box or crate. Sometimes the box moved and the sailor quickly drew back. Uttering an exclamation about being bitten or scratched, he moved aside for the next viewer. Slowly, the new men were sucked in. As each bent to look into the hole he was soundly smacked with a broom handle across his upraised backside. Everyone had a good laugh then quieted until the next landlubber came along. The new initiate, embarrassed at being taken by such an obvious ruse, generally joined in the joke and stayed to watch the next round. You can get away with this only once if a group of new men showed up together. When that happened there was jostling and banter among the sailors to reach a general agreement as to who should be allowed to go first. The civilians were always given head-of-the-line privileges! Most were good sports, taking their hits and laughing when it was over.

In one unforgettable instance a young, serious Ph.D. came aft, was taken into the con and got his shot across the ass. He jumped up, looked around, muttered something about trying to see the bat, bent over, and got nailed a second time. He rose, angrier this time, confronted his attacker and demanded the sailor stop hitting him. Unbelievably, he bent and looked into the box a third time. *CRACK!!* This time with real vigor. It must have stung fiercely. His face grew red! Approaching rage, he shouted if he wasn't going to be allowed to see the thing in peace, then he didn't care about the damned seabat! Abruptly leaving the fantail, he stormed forward along the port side. The crew broke into an uproar. People laughed so hard tears squeezed from their eyes. Never before in the history of seabat hunting had anyone taken three hits. It was hilarious!

Someone must have clued him in later. It would be sad to think that a young man could go through life that humorless and that naive. Of course, the merciless sailors did not let him forget the incident for the rest of the cruise.

SET THE SEA AND ANCHOR DETAIL

BY DAVE HOOD

Destroyermen can be rather elitist. Snobbish, even. When naval action is called for, be it combat, recovering a downed pilot, rescuing survivors of a shipwreck, a destroyer is usually first on the scene and the last to leave. They have a *can do* attitude. When I told my parents that I drew duty onboard a destroyer, my stepfather, a WWII Marine, told me that he was delighted by that choice. He said that he had noticed that destroyermen had a certain cavalier arrogance to them. They bode of confidence and were the personification of *esprit de corps*. I think the term "cocky" is quite accurate.

Not much impresses a destroyerman. SEALS, F-4 pilots, Israeli soldiers, astronauts (the old ones, not those new Space Shuttle ones), Marine Gunnery Sergeants and Jamie Lee Curtis might impress a destroyerman, but not much else. Certainly not supply ships, aircraft carriers, amphibs, tugboats, frigates or the entire United States Coast Guard. Especially not frigates. We hated frigates, and we took pity on the sailors who served on them.

We referred to the *Knox*-class FF as "half a ship" or

"congressional yacht." We mocked their single 5-inch gun mount, their twin boilers, their single screw and their top speed of only twenty-seven knots. Real ships, like a *Gearing*-class DD, had at least four 5-inch guns, four boilers, twin screws, twin rudders, a thirty-five plus knots speed, and best of all, they didn't need a stinkin' tugboat to get in and out of port!

In March and April of '78, the *USS McKean (DD-784)* was in SoCal waters for REFTRA. On the 21st of March we refueled off the *USS Wichita (AOR-1)*. We again refueled off her on the 22nd. We pulled into La Playa for fuel and ammo on the 31st. On the 4th of April, we unrepped off the *USS Constellation (CV-64)*. We gassed up at Point Loma on the 7th. On the 10th we unrepped from the *USNS Taluga (AO-62)*. We finished REFTRA on 11 April with a passing score. We pulled into 32nd Street for a deserved overnight liberty. On the 12th we set the Sea and Anchor detail and steamed from 32nd Street to Point Loma.

We moored portside with our stern facing the open sea. There, we gassed up and took on 5-inch ammo and six warshot ASROC missiles. Our next stop was home, Seattle, with a liberty stop in Eureka, California on the way. We were tired, homesick and horny.

Just as we were ready to set the Sea and Anchor detail to get underway, a *Knox*-class frigate pulled up...with a tug. We lined the rails, chewed tobacco (a Sea and Anchor tradition aboard the *McKean*) and watched the tedious method in which the FF parked in front of us, its bow facing the sea. When its lines were on the pier, the tug cast off and maneuvered over towards us. Our CO, Commander Larry Smith, had a fit. "Get that $!@"*& tug away from my destroyer! No %&$(*&% tug is going to touch my ship!" He waved the tug away and we singled up all lines. With Capt. Smith still yelling at the tug, we took in lines two, three, four and five, and finally, line six.

The starboard engine was signaled to go forward and the port engine reverse. The rudder was cranked to starboard and line one was brought aboard. The stern pivoted away from the pier and the rudder was placed amidships and both engines were placed into reverse. With more distance gained from the pier, the starboard engine was signaled forward and we spun one hundred and eighty degrees along the length of the FF. With our bow now pointed out to sea, we came up alongside of her, perhaps no more then fifty feet separating us. We were close enough to the *Knox*-class to see that her line handlers were standing on the port side of their ship amazed at this display of maneuverability. To further impress them as to what a real warship could do, Captain Smith ordered, "All ahead two-thirds!" The look on their faces confirmed that they were astonished at our speed. And to completely impress them with our *esprit de corps* and cavalier attitude, STGSN Piper rendered them honors by going to the stern and mooning them just as we passed their bridge.

The frigate's CO wasn't so impressed. He sent a message to Captain Smith and lodged a protest over being mooned. The duty MAA quickly identified Piper as the guilty party - he was the one grinning and we were the ones rolling on the deck laughing. Piper was taken straight to the bridge and disciplined on the spot. He was confined to the ship for 48 hours. Two days and two hours later, we pulled into Eureka, California for one of the best liberties ever.

OUT OF THE FRYING PAN

BY BOB COHEN

Even in San Diego, it wasn't very often that the Navy was on network television, so when the teaser for the six o'clock news announced that there was an upcoming story featuring one of our sister ships, every TV set on the *Henry B. Wilson* was standing-room only.

The lead story turned out to be about a couple of errant bluejackets from the *USS John Doe*. It seems they were nabbed by the San Diego cops while ineptly trying to steal a sailboat. Hardly newsworthy, really, just typical drunken beach shenanigans. Well, that is except for one minor detail: when they were collared, they also had in their possession a whole bunch of other stolen property – pistols, shotguns, rifles and even an M-60 machine gun – all belonging to the *USS John Doe*. To make matters worse, they'd been over the hill for quite some time (which the newscasters made sure to point out) and apparently nobody on the *Doe* had noticed the distinct lack of clutter in the small-arms locker. Oh, boy.

What the circumstances were behind this particular escapade and where exactly those guys were going with all that artillery remained a mystery to us. Right around the same time, though, the scuttlebutt was that one of Ronald Reagan's six-hundred ship fleet was imminently going to be deployed to somewhere off the coast of Nicaragua. Possibly just coincidence, but the most likely contender had been the *Doe* – or so the story went.

One bright and sunny day not too long afterwards, I was standing inport watch as duty engineer. I was topside, discussing rumors and other important naval matters with the officer of the deck when we spotted a familiar silhouette passing under the Coronado Bridge, coming south towards us. The beautiful lines of the *Adams*-class guided missile destroyer were unmistakable. It was our sister ship, the *USS John Doe*.

We were in the last berth on the end of one of the northern-most piers, with the rest of the sprawling 32nd Street Naval Station south of us. As the *Doe* approached, we could see that she was flying that yellow flag with the black circle indicating that she was done for the day. She was moving at a good clip, maybe ten knots or so. We were a little puzzled since we figured she'd be tying up next to us. The OOD said, "Wonder where they're going …" There were plenty of empty parking spots on our pier but it looked like she was definitely headed somewhere else. Then, unexpectedly, the *Doe* smartly came left, bearing directly down our pier. Neither one of us took our eyes off her as I said, "They're coming in a little fast, aren't they?" Sailors from the *Wilson* lined the rails as the *Doe* flashed by us. "Oh, yeah."

We never heard any collision alarm, but to be fair, we did see her screws bite as she backed down hard – only about two ship-lengths from the shore end of the pier. I said to the OOD, "I think we better call away our repair party," as I wondered what would happen when the irresistible force (a four-thousand ton warship) met the immovable object (California).

If you want to know what it sounded like, just ask any bubble-head who was on ballistic missile patrol underneath the polar icecap, because I'm sure they heard it out there, too. It was an impossibly long and deep *"KARRRUUUNCCCHHHH."*

Our Command Duty Officer rushed topside as soon as he heard our alarm directing the *Wilson's* damage-control people to muster on the pier. Judging from the way the light hurt his eyes (and the pillow scars on his face) it was obvious we had interrupted his plan-of-the-day. "What's going on?" The OOD and I were both grinning like idiots: "You're not gonna believe this, but the *Doe* just hit the quay wall at about ten knots!" And there she was, where no destroyer belonged, bow down in an enormous hissing cloud of shore steam and concrete dust. The CDO rubbed his eyes and said, "Well, I guess everybody'll stop talking about the guns now."

S'POSTWERK

BY TERRY L. MILLER

The *USS George K MacKenzie (DD-836)* was 23 years old in the summer of 1968 and like any ship of that age, it had an accumulation of gear that was no longer used. In fact, the *GKM* had some gear that no one could remember what its use had been. Other equipment might be used, but not necessarily by the people responsible for the space where it was located. And once in a while, as Henry Fonda said in the movie *In Harm's Way*, while the Navy is never wrong, it was a mite short on being right. Such was the case with the Dead Reckoning Indicator in the Mighty Mack's Sonar Control.

I was a Sonar Technician striker when I was introduced to the S'postwerk. That's "supposed to work" run together like a single word of two syllables. At least that's how Marv pronounced it.

Marv, the ship's Weapons Officer, wasn't named Marv but always said, "marvelous" when he really liked something or if he really didn't like it. Marvelous!

"You didn't get that job done on time like I told you? Well, that's just marvelous." Or, "This Division got a perfect score on our last inspection. Marvelous!" See? Didn't matter. It was marvelous so he became Marv.

Anyway, Marv wanted to know what the Dead Reckoning Indicator (DRI) was. Frequently. In fact, every time he entered Sonar Control he asked me the same question.

"What's that?"

"It's a DRI, sir."

"What's it do?"

"Holds up the pubs locker, sir." Our publications locker was really a small safe for storing Sonar's classified pubs. It was attached to the thin aluminum bulkhead immediately above the DRI. The bottom of the safe sat directly on top of the DRI.

"What else?"

"Nothing, sir."

"What? Why not?"

"Because it doesn't work, sir."

At this point, one of my two ST1 bosses, Andy Anderson, was desperately looking for something to do to take his mind off the conversation. Mostly so he wouldn't be blamed. The other one, Ben Harris, heard his grandmother calling or something, and left.

"Why doesn't it work?" Marv may have had a short memory or else he really didn't pay attention.

"Because when they moved it from the other side of CIC over to this bulkhead they put it on the wrong side. It's here in Sonar but it belongs out there in CIC."

"Well, it's spostwerk. And even if it's here, it's still spostwerk."

This was pronounced as the single word I already told you about. "Why didn't CIC have it moved to their side of the bulkhead?"

"This is a secure space, sir. They can't come in so they don't know it's here. Besides, they don't use the one they have, either."

"They have another one? Why?"

"I guess the Navy thought they needed one and since they didn't have one after this one was moved in here, somebody at the yards ordered them another one, but they don't use it because it isn't accurate enough."

Now Marv knows Dead Reckoning is the least reliable method of figuring out where you are, but he won't let go of his train of thought. He would remind you of a small dog with a mouthful of your pants leg except that Marv didn't growl.

"Well, why don't you use it then?"

"Because it isn't accurate enough for our needs, either."

"Well, it's here and it's spostwerk." His level of frustration is really beginning to show by now.

"How do you get position reports if you don't use this?"

"I stick my head out the door and ask CIC." Marv had to walk past the position chart table in CIC to get into Sonar Control in the first place. It was less than six feet from our door.

The final outcome was that two IC electricians spent four days mad at me for telling Marv that it didn't work and forcing them to fix the thing. They told him that it probably couldn't be fixed but it took the rest of the week before Marv gave up and got it removed. I reminded him that before he had it removed we were going to need a bracket to hold up the pubs locker.

BATTLESHIP OHIO

BY KEN DANDURAND

Note: This is an excerpt from Ken's Master's thesis in History. While his original work also included extensive photos and charts which are beyond the scope of this book, this excerpt serves to illustrate an amazing and little-known connection between battleships and destroyers - one that might have been forever lost if not for Ken's diligent research and insight. The Publisher gratefully acknowledges permission given by the faculty of the School of American History, Colorado Southwestern University at Reina Mercedes, to reprint this here –Ed.

History of the USS Ohios
Ohio was admitted to the Union 1 March 1803, as the 17th State.

I
The first *Ohio* was a merchant schooner.
Purchased by the Navy in 1812; converted to a warship by Henry Eckford; and commissioned prior to 13 June 1813, Sailing Master Daniel Dobbins in command.
Ohio served on Lake Erie in the squadron commanded by Captain Oliver H. Perry during the War of 1812. On 12 August 1824, she was captured with *Somers* by the British within pistol shot of Fort Erie.

II
The second *Ohio* was a gunboat.
(Ship-of-the-line: tonnage 2,724; length 197'; beam 53'; depth of hold 22'2"; complement 840; armament 12 8", 7 32-pounders)
Designed by Henry Eckford, *Ohio* was laid down at New York Navy Yard in 1817 and launched 30 May 1820. She went into ordinary [discontinued service] and in the ensuing years decayed badly. Refitted for service in 1838, *Ohio* sailed 16 October 1838 to join the Mediterranean Squadron under Commodore Isaac Hull. Acting as flagship for two years, she protected commerce and suppressed the slave trade off the African coast. *Ohio* proved to be an excellent

sea-boat repeatedly making more than 12 knots. One of her officers stated, "I never supposed such a ship could be built — a ship possessing in so great a degree all the qualifications of a perfect vessel." In 1840 *Ohio* returned to Boston where she again went into ordinary. From 1841 to 1846 *Ohio* served as receiving ship.

To meet the needs of the Mexican War, *Ohio* was recommissioned 7 December 1846 and sailed 4 January 1847 for the Gulf of Mexico, arriving off Vera Cruz 22 March. *Ohio* landed 10 guns on 27 March to help in the siege of Vera Cruz, but the city soon surrendered.

In 1850 she returned to Boston where she again went into ordinary. In 1851, *Ohio* became receiving ship and continued this duty until again placed in ordinary in 1875. *Ohio* was sold at Boston to J. L. Snow of Rockland, Maine 27 September 1883.

III

The third *Ohio* was a battleship.

(Battleship BB-12, *Maine*-class: displacement 12,723 tons; length 393'10"; beam 72'3"; draft 23'10"; speed 18 knots; complement 561; armament 4 12", 16 6", 6 3", 8 3-pounders, 6 1-pounders, 2 .30 caliber machine guns)

The third *Ohio (BB-12)* was laid down 22 April 1899 by Union Iron Works, San Francisco, Calif.; launched 18 May 1901; sponsored by Miss Helen Deschler; and commissioned 4 October 1904, Captain Leavitt C. Logan in command.

Designated flagship of the Asiatic Fleet, *Ohio* departed San Francisco 1 April 1905 for Manila, where she embarked the party of then Secretary of War William Howard Taft, which included Miss Alice Roosevelt, the President's daughter. She conducted this party on much of its Far Eastern tour of inspection, and continued the cruise in Japanese, Chinese and Philippine waters until returning to the United States in 1907.

Ohio sailed out of Hampton Roads, Va., 16 December 1907 with the battleships of the Atlantic Fleet. Guns crashed a salute to President Theodore Roosevelt while he reviewed the Great White Fleet as it began the cruise around the world which, perhaps more than any other event, marked the emergence of the United States as a major world power.

Commanded by Rear Admiral Robley D. Evans, and later, Rear Admiral Charles S. Sperry, the fleet made calls on the east and west coasts of South America, rounding the Horn in between, en route to San Francisco. On 7 July 1908, *Ohio* and her sisters shaped their course west to Hawaii, New Zealand and Australia. On each visit the American ships were welcomed with great enthusiasm but none of their ports of call received them with such enthusiastic friendliness as Tokyo where they anchored 18 October. The fleet's presence in Japan symbolized both American friendship and strength and helped to ease dangerously strained relations between the two countries.

The fleet put in at Amoy, returned to Yokohama, held target practice in the Philippines and was homeward-bound 1 December. After steaming through the Suez Canal 4 January 1909, the fleet made Mediterranean calls, before anchoring in Hampton Roads 22 February.

Ohio sailed on to New York, her home port for the next 4 years during duty training men of the New York Naval Militia and performing general service with the Atlantic Fleet.

The *USS Ohio (BB-12)* was decommissioned 31 May 1922; and was sold for scrapping 24 March 1923. During her years of service she circumnavigated the globe three times, and was the subject of an unusual occurrence that sends shivers all along any ship's keel. (Dandurand, *op. cit.,* 16-18)

IV

A fourth *Ohio (BB-68)* was authorized 19 July 1940 and her construction assigned to the Philadelphia Navy Yard. Construction was cancelled 21 July 1943.

V

The fifth *Ohio* is the *USS Ohio (SSBN-726)*. It is the first *Trident*-class and is a ballistic missile submarine and still in service.

USS OHIO (BB-12) and The Borken Canal
By Kenneth Dandurand

Soon after the United States entered World War I, the *USS Ohio* was sent to the Mediterranean to protect our interests in the region. On February 24th 1916, the *Ohio* was called upon to provide gun support and maneuverability of the US Navy in support of the Allied invasion of Croatia and the opposing Serbian supporters of the Kaiser that were entrenched there.

The *Ohio* sailed up the Gulf of Venice in the Adriatic sea, down between the islands and the mainland and into the Borken Canal that ran from near Saline to Novigrad. There she moved about in the Dalmatia Sea and provided heavy gun support for the French and British units that were advancing there.

The unusual part of the trip was on the 25th of February. The *Ohio* was halfway up the Borken Canal when the Serbs blew up the cliffs near Jesenice and cut off the flow of water down the canal. Quick thinking on behalf of then-Captain William Neel was to become one of the marvels of Navy engineering. When the water started to subside, the *Ohio* was at the Borken Locks, the second set of locks in the canal. The canal ahead became dry and the *Ohio* was indeed in a troubling spot. Landlocked some four miles from sea and three and-a-half miles from her destination and with hills on either side of her, she was a proverbial sitting duck for the Kaiser's biplanes and their bombs.

Captain Neel had the local workers and his sailors form a rail through the docks and the canal to the Dalmatia Sea using wooden dunnage that was being shipped to England for use in her docks. Utilizing the power of horses, cattle and the ships' crew and local laborers, the *Ohio* was inched slowly yet methodically up the canal and into the locks of the Dalmatia Sea. There her boilers were re-lit and she again got underway on a full head of steam.

The *Ohio* provided gunfire support for the Allied invasion group and drove the Serbs from the hills surrounding the waterways and the highway now known as E-80. The *Ohio* sailed around the Dalmatia Sea for two weeks in waters that had never been charted and in depths that had not been established, yet never once ran aground.

While the *Ohio* provided the needed support, the British engineers of Her Majesty's Ulster Engineers re-opened the dammed waterway and again there was water flowing through the canal.

Relieved in more ways than one, the *Ohio* made haste in exiting the Dalmatia Sea and the Borken Canal and headed happily out into the Mediterrancan Sea. She was allowed to stand down in Gibraltar for a week, then was sent back into the Mediterranean to carry on her support of the Allies.

A year later, Captain Neel was advanced to Admiral by President Roosevelt, in person, at ceremonies in Annapolis, his Alma Mater.

Three years later, Admiral Neel, then retired, was made Chief of Engineers, the leading position for the Corps of Engineers, largely due to his engineering skills while Commanding Officer of the *USS Ohio.*

THE CHRISTMAS BEAR

BY KEN DANDURAND

Back in 1985 I wanted a part-time job since we had just purchased a new home and a new car. Having lived on a farm as a child, I applied at the Flying W Ranch just west of Colorado Springs adjacent to the Garden of the Gods. The Flying W is a working ranch, but also is a country and western restaurant. It is one of the only types of it's kind in the world. It sits nestled in a valley and the one hillside is a maze of pathways that go to Teepees where real Indians make real blankets on real looms. It goes to a small "Walnut Grove"-type church where they do weddings. It goes to the jail, several shops, and a cabin.

When people show up at 6 p.m. in the summer they wander through, and buy shirts, candies, jams, etc. that the Flying W sells. At 8 p.m. they are herded down to the indoor or outdoor theatre (depending on weather conditions). There, the same people that they have previously seen in the teepee, stores, etc., feed them in record time. The people (up to 1400) are fed in less than twenty minutes. Then they are treated to a one-hour show of country and western i.e., Ol' dogie, mission bells, horse and range songs by the second-oldest country band in the US of A. The other claim to fame is the red beans that they serve. They are the second (formerly first) purveyor of red beans in America. Only Wendy's Restaurants buys and sells more. Also on site is the Steakhouse.

The steakhouse is an old theater, formerly the UTE Theater in Colorado Springs. It was torn down and reassembled on the ranch. In the winter it is the only heated building on the site. I started working there the end of August when they open and use the Steakhouse.

I sold tickets to the customers as they arrived, bussed tables and washed dishes. When I was done with the dishes and had them all stacked and put away, I was all alone on the show side of the ranch. My final job was to turn out all lights on the hillside and leave, locking the gate at the entrance. The only problem was the last light switch was way up the side of the hill. The good side was that the path went straight down and across the front of the buildings to the parking lot. The other bad part was the location. In the valley, when the lights are turned out, it is dark like you have never experienced. Any that have camped in a valley know what I mean. There are stars visible above, but as far as seeing in front of you? Forget it. I usually took a flashlight with me, but this time I did not.

When I got to the final light switch, I got my bearings and flipped it off, and immediately felt the hair on the back of my head stand on end. I felt like somebody, something was watching me. I reached for the switch and flipped it back on. I looked around, but saw nothing. I called out, but no one answered. Again, I turned out the light and started walking down the path. I had this scary feeling so I walked a little faster. Thinking that there may be people who were left after the show, I started singing out loud. I think it was, "Jesus loves me, this I know." You know, just in case my presence might startle someone. Now I am on the paved sidewalk that runs out to the parking lot, and see no reason on earth why I shouldn't jog to the car. By the time I get to the ticket booth area, I am at a dead run. Yes, I was scared.

In the parking lot just outside the ticket booth they have a big yellow wagon that sits directly between two big ponderosa pines. One tree sits by the tongue of the wagon, and the other sits just behind the wagon. It was placed there by a crane and would have to be taken out the same way.

Just as I cleared the ticket office/entrance, the bear came down the tree directly in front of me. At a dead run, I could not even stop, so I veered to the right and headed for the car. I could hear the bear growl. When I glanced back, he WAS coming after me. Now I am scared to shit. I got by the car and knew that if I stopped, I would never get the door unlocked and get inside before he got to me, so I bounded over the hood and kept on going toward the front gate and Colorado Springs.

By now, my ears are attuned to the grunts that the bear was making as he chased after me. I didn't stop at the gate either. I headed straight down the road and ran for all I was worth. About a mile and a half down the road I had had it. I decided that whatever was going to happen was going to happen right here, and right now.

I stopped and sat on one of the logs that lined the road. I just put my head between my knees and tried to get oxygen into my body. It took precedence over fear. My body needed oxygen.

Then I heard him. He was right beside me, wheezing and breathing as loud as I was. He looked up at me and said "Ken …"

I am serious. He was a talking bear. Honest to God. He looked at me and said, "Gotta catch my breath, then I'm gonna eat you." If you are wondering how he knew my name, just remember, he was watching me for three months before he attacked me.

As we both sat there sucking in the mountain air, he said, "If you got away, no one would believe you anyway."

I said, "You are wrong. There are always people who will believe almost anything that one says or writes!"

"No!" says the bear, "people aren't that dumb."

"Oh yeah?" says I, "I wrote a story about the USS Ohio going through a canal on railroad tracks, to a lake to shoot at the enemy and they all believed it."

"So, you see, people will believe anything."

Life at Sea

KNOX CLASS

Length: 438' Displacement: 3020 tons 46 built, in service 1969-1994

MMC Robert teGroen
M Division, USS Gray (FF-1054) 1981-82*

MIDN 1/c Bob Cohen
Engineering Department, USS Whipple (FF-1062) 1980**

(* Selected Reserves ** temporary additional duty)

WHAT ARE THOSE ANIMALS DOING DOWN THERE?

BY ROBERT TEGROEN

Most non-snipes on tin cans walked by the four engineering hatches, getting pasted by a blast of hot air and noise several times a day and I wondered if that's what they asked themselves: what are those animals doing down there? After all, that's what I asked myself when I passed by the radio room, sonar, etc. For myself, my descent into Hades (forward or after engineroom) made me feel quite at home and comfortable; I was home and content in my element. When the night orders called for getting underway at 0800 from a *cold iron* pierside berth, I looked forward to bringing the steam engine to life and making the 2200-plus tons of destroyer come to life, on her own, and move.

Unlike an automobile that is *internal combustion*, steam engines are *external combustion*, so the driving force for the engine is somewhere other than where the engine is.

Hence the BTs were up first, usually around 0400, and after venting the boiler and opening the steam drains, a fire is lit on one of the burners using a long metal pole with a burning rag on the end, and with the call, "Fire in the Hole!" steam is raised. The procedure in both firerooms and enginerooms is to bring the pressure and temperatures up slowly, not stressing the steam lines and especially the brickwork of the boilers.

My arrival in the engineroom with the lighting-off crew an hour or so later always impressed me with the *sleeping giant* feeling. Here was 30,000 horsepower waiting to be unleashed and it was my job to make it happen. It was usually very quiet, just a single ventilation blower going but that was about to change. So what was the premier important job that had to be done? Get the coffee pot perking, stupid!

By the time I arrived the BTs had enough pressure in the boiler to operate the steam-driven pumps so we opened the auxiliary steam line drains and started warming up. We also opened up the main steam line bypass valves so the main steam lines could warm up slowly. First came the main circulating pump, main condensate pump, and the air ejectors to raise vacuum in the condenser. Isn't that an oxymoron, to "raise" vacuum? Next came the main lube oil pump, and as my MM school ten commandants said, "The world turneth endlessly on its bearings without oil but not so thy engine room machinery; ensure clean oil to thy engine bearings."

At that time the jacking gear was engaged and the turbine blades rotated so that they would not become warped by uneven heating. The turbine gland sealing system was also started so that the turbine shafts were sealed. By this time additional supply and exhaust fans were in operation contributing to the noise level. Next in operation was the main feed booster pump and then the main feed pump to supply the boiler so that the BTs could secure their reciprocating feed pump. Then the ship's service turbo-generator was lined up and lit off exhausting to the auxiliary condenser. Later the electricians would put the SSTG on line and the pierside supply disconnected. Later the SSTG exhaust would be shifted to the main condenser.

Shortly before the time for getting underway, the main steam valves are opened admitting steam to the turbine throttle valves and the jacking gear disconnected. Permission is then requested from the OOD to spin main engines, (without making way on the ship). After testing main engines the turbines are spun every five minutes to avoid warping the turbine blades.

About this time the evaporator man is lighting off the evaps, after all we've been dumping condensate into the bilges during the lighting off process and the pierside water supply has been disconnected, so we need to make water, mainly feed water. By the way, do you recall that the water shortage mainly occurred in port while not tied up to a pier? That's because an evaporator boils water under a vacuum and at much less than 212 degrees temp. So while the ship is at anchor, the evaporator is sucking up seawater and the brown lumps from the heads. It makes great feed water for the boilers but nothing I want to drink or take a shower in. That's why the order of the day was, *"No Hollywood Showers!"* (oryoullbestandingthemidwatch-ontheevapstonite).

Finally, after testing the engine order telegraph we report to the bridge, "Ready to answer all bells." Another fun time in snipe country.

(Reference: *Operation Manual, Main Propulsion Plant, DD445 and DD692 classes, Destroyers and Converted Types.* U.S. Navy Bureau of Ships, Revision 2. NAVSHIPS 341-5506. Oct. 1952.)

NARRAGANSETT BAY DEPARTURE

BY MIKE SNYDER

We had taken on fuel, food and water in preparation for a short excursion into the local op-area. This was to be a Navy-only cruise for independent exercises. *USS Glover (AGDE-1)* had the capacity to berth up to 35 civilians without impinging on crew comfort, but there were no civilian engineer-scientists scheduled aboard for this trip. The former ASROC and torpedo magazines, now berthing spaces, echoed dully with their absence.

It was a spectacular Northeast morning. As the Engineering Department BTs and MMs boarded, the air was perfectly still. It was chilly enough to wear jackets and a light fog floated above the mirror smooth surface of Narragansett Bay at Newport. The engineers reported aboard early to light off the boilers, get up steam, generate electricity, switch over to ship's power, and otherwise make ready for getting underway. The remainder of the crew straggled aboard in little groups deferring to the 0700 curfew. Everyone shifted into the uniform of the day, and reported directly to their Sea and Anchor Detail stations. Muster was taken on station and passed to the bridge along with departmental and divisional readiness for getting underway reports. We shifted colors before 0800.

With a scream that mimicked the sounds of a Boeing 707 jet, our teapot-shaped, pressure-fired boilers answered a "Back Two-Thirds" bell and we ghosted out into the mist. A few wives and kids waved listlessly from the pier. They knew we'd be back in a few days.

The *Glover* backed slowly out of Coddington Cove in the long, wide arc to port characteristic of all USN single-screw ships. It made getting underway from a pier relatively easy but destroyed many well intentioned landings. The bright sun quickly burned away the mist and the sky moderated from pink to a hard, almost painful blue. Jackets came off while the mooring lines were wound on reels and the fenders were hauled aboard.

Engine Stop. Ahead one third. That was it. Three bells and we were headed fair, angling out into the ship channel toward the open sea. The noise from the boiler compressors settled to a low moan accentuated by excursions into higher ranges as the automatic combustion control system (ACC) modified the steaming rate to accommodate small changes in engineering plant settings. In all, it was a fine navy day.

Passing easily under the Newport Bridge suspension span, the *Glover* headed into the narrow, rock strewn channel that connected the bay and the sea. Turning slightly left at Rose Island, the ship pointed directly at Old Fort Adams leaving "The Dumplings" to starboard. A hard right carried us safely under Castle Hill where families frequently wave their final goodbyes, then out between Brenton Point on our left and Beaver Tail on the right. We eased into one last left turn that would see us past the Brenton Reef light and out into deep water.

The day that had begun so idyllically was suddenly interrupted by alarms. From my station on the fantail I recognized the gyro alarm ringing on the bridge. Other bells and horns sounded throughout the ship. The incessant whistle and shriek from our stacks lost its hard edge, then subsided to a whisper as the combustion-air turbines spun down. The urgent alarms were silenced one by one as watchstanders and roving patrols pressed buttons or threw switches. In a few minutes all was quiet.

Going dead-in-the-water in a combatant is an eerie experience. Ships are filled with motors, pumps, fans, engines, transformers, compressors, and generators all humming and singing with their particular sound. The crew grows accustomed to the noise and it becomes background, a part of the web of shipboard life. With power lost, all the voices go quiet. The silence is deafening. Instinctively sailors know when it's quiet aboard ship something is very wrong. Within the skin of the ship it is not only quiet, but dark. Dimly glowing, battery powered emergency lamps replace the bright white lights. Spoken words seem especially loud in the noise-void. You can hear people running and calling throughout the ship as they rush to control stations to isolate equipment and repair their particular problem.

Headway fell off and the *Glover* was soon adrift in the ship channel at the entrance to Narragansett Bay. This morning, fortunately, there was no other traffic threatening to run over us. We lay within a mile or two of the rocks on both sides. A slight breeze was blowing from the east and the tide was slack.

The *Garcia* and *Brooke* classes of destroyer escorts, of which the *Glover* was one, were built with a positive displacement fuel system to maintain stability. As fuel is consumed, sea water is drawn into the tanks to replace it. When fuel is taken on sea water is displaced overboard. The act of fueling, however, creates a problem. The water - oil interface is disturbed and it takes many hours, tending toward days, to settle out. This morning, our engineers had aligned a newly-filled tank to the boilers and taken water into the fuel system. When the water hit the boilers, the fires went out and the automatic combustion controls (ACC) shut down the steam generating plant. In other steam ships it is a fairly straight forward process of clearing fuel lines of water, lining up a new tank and refiring the boilers. But not in a pressure-fired ship. You first need electricity to spin up a combustion-air compressor to support boiler fires.

To get electricity in a cold-iron ship you need a generator. Generators are turned by diesel engines. Diesel engines are started with compressed air from flasks. And there lay a problem more basic than losing fires. There was no air in the diesel generator starting-air flasks. Without air, there was no diesel engine, to turn the generator to provide the electricity, to spin the compressor, to supply the air, to start the fires, to make the steam, to turn the turbine, to power the ship.

From the fo'c'sle, the heavy clunk of anchor chain could be heard. The captain had ordered the anchor walked out on the brake in hopes of finding bottom and preventing the ship from drifting ashore. Black cone and ball day shapes showing limited maneuverability were hoisted on the signal halyards. These are commonly referred to as *breakdown* signals. We were embarrassed at the entrance to our home port.

The *Glover* was scheduled to conduct gunfire exercises during this outing. In the days prior to getting underway, the gunner's mates had filled two 6-foot long, 2-foot diameter air flasks with 3000 PSI air. One supported the gun recoil system; the second provided back-up charging air for launching torpedoes from their tubes.

When we learned the solution to the ship's dilemma was starting air, my gunner's mates contacted A-gang and informed them of the filled flasks. Together they devised a method to route the high pressure air to the diesel generator. It took the better part of an hour to line up the piping. Soon after, the wheeze of an air starter was heard, followed by belches of blue smoke, then the steady roar of an 8-cylinder diesel. We were making progress.

The electricians stripped the main switchboard of its load, brought the generator on line and slowly began to restore power to electrical circuits. One by one the alarms that sounded when power was lost resumed their insistent clangor and were silenced by watchstanders. Lights blinked on throughout the ship. With power restored the boiler techs initiated their dance to bring the boilers up to steaming again. Topside, the morning was interrupted by the noise of the blowers as they spun up and rammed air into the teapots. A smoke plume poured from the stacks; first white then black. Another hour passed before the ship could be maneuvered. Carefully we backed away from the shore at Beaver Tail and picked up the anchor. The day shapes were hauled and the *Glover* got underway again for the open sea. She had lain exposed and cold, threatened by the shore, for nearly three hours. Without further incident we conducted our scheduled exercises and returned to Newport later in the week.

There was no great fanfare aboard the *Glover*, but everyone knew the gunner's mates had, this day, saved the collective asses of all her engineers. The alternative scenario to this dilemma was a tow into port behind a tug at the end of a wire. Potentially an ignominious end to what actually turned out to be a great time underway.

NO PURPLE HEARTS

BY ROBERT TEGROEN

Since the invention of the ship I don't think they or the sea have ever been without hazard to one's body. From the days of sail comes the adage, "One hand for the ship, one hand for yourself," and it's still true and probably why I got chewed out for having both hands in my pockets in boot camp.

I'm only aware of one close encounter with the enemy and I learned of it some hours later when I was informed that the *USS Ernest G. Small (DDR-838)* had been challenged by a Chinese radar station up in the Yellow Sea while we were partaking of the Korean War in 1953. Not wanting to engage in a gun duel we ran, I'm told. As usual I was asleep at the time, as I was days later when I was awakened at night by loud banging on the deck above our compartment. Several men left the compartment to check on the noise so I went back to sleep, that's probably what happened on the *Maine*; I've read it also happened on the *Royal Oak* at Scapa Flow, a small jolt or bang, oh well, go back to sleep. Seems a depth charge had gotten loose and was playing hockey on the weather deck, and it took several people some time to get it back in its cradle. Don't those things go * *BOOOOM!* * doing that?

Diet has killed and disabled more sailors than enemy action, I've read. Scurvy killed many in the early years but the English found that lime juice (vitamin C) kept it in check. In '53 I would watch the medical department inspect the Japanese veggies being hauled aboard up one side and then being tossed over the side into the garbage barge on the other side, and was told they were slimy or dirty or something like that. So we ate what we had. Then I developed a large boil on the back of my right hand that became quite painful and ended up having it lanced (a very good job by the medicine man, I might add). But maybe if I had taken my vitamins I wouldn't have had a problem. At least the boil wasn't on my butt.

My next adventure with personal injury (and I'm excluding the usual shin and head hematomas from hatches, and the casual application of hot steam pipes to a snipe's anatomy) was during an ACDUTRA on the *USS Vammen (DE-644).* I was injury prone, I think, on this ship. We had spent a couple days in San Diego's damage control training tank, getting soaked, and then had to wait in a cold wind for the bus. After a couple of days back at sea I came down with what the Doc described as bronchitis after he heard me coughing. The cough started somewhere down below my navel and rumbled up through the lungs; actually I think it was "the big P," but he took me off watch and I spent several days in my rack taking pills and resting. God bless Doc Fox.

On another *Vammen* cruise we had been at sea for several days, and after a great navy lunch I went topside and flaked out on the main deck. It was warm, maybe very warm. I had, attached to my bell-bottom's belt, a special knife I used for cutting pump packing, and I had sharpened this blade to a fine sharpness while standing top watch. It was an unusual knife, I can only explain it as being a "sheepshead" shape, most of the blade exposed while folded and only the edge shielded. The knife was suspended from my pants by a halyard snap on my right side and starting at my belt, it would be snap, knife body, blade, *if* opened.

I awoke sometime later realizing I was hot and groggy from the deck heat so I tried to stand up. Something was holding me down so I got pissed and jerked upright. WRONG. My right hand had been on that exposed sheepshead blade and it unfolded perfectly so as to lacerate my palm from the inside right wrist all the way to the center of my palm. I had never been awake when so much red blood gushed from my body at one time, but by applying direct pressure I slowed it and managed to find the corpsman's bunk (he was napping too), and kicking him soundly awake, showed him my bloody appendage.

A good wrapping of bandage stanched the flow, and we made port in San Diego where the corpsmen at the base hospital vied and pleaded for the privilege of sewing up my wound. I insisted that a *real* doctor do the deed and I finally prevailed. This was also the first time I got a large dose of demerol and I recall floating out of the hospital like a balloon on a string back to the ship, being towed by the doc. Despite an infection of the wound and nerves that took a long time to recover (I still have problems with typing, my little finger is deformed) I was left with just a big scar on my palm. "It don't slow down a snipe."

And then (I promise this is the last), one morning I was descending the *Vammen's* engineroom by myself to light off. In my left hand I had logs, in my mouth I had logs, in my right hand I had a cup of galley coffee. Well, I had descended this vertical ladder many times but this time I stepped off about two rungs too early. My right foot turned under and inward and I fell in a heap, coffee and logs in all directions. After rolling around in pain for several minutes I finally got upright and proceeded to limp around and get things humming. But the ankle never healed from the sprain (and it's not in my navy medical records) and I've sprained it at least 10 times since because it was so weak, so that I'm paying for it now with arthritis. My bone doctor says, "Gee! Arthritis usually doesn't attack a joint unless it's been injured." Thanks, Doc.

And of course there was an investigation of my knife incident, probably suspecting I had been in a knife fight, but I had to confess it was only a stupid personal accident. The damned knife is somewhere on the bottom of the ocean where I threw it on the way back to Long Beach.

GULF STREAM RESCUE

BY MIKE SNYDER

The destroyer had recently come out of the Philadelphia Naval Shipyard and, following an upkeep period in Norfolk, was enroute to Guantanamo Bay, Cuba for refresher training. We steamed down the east coast of the United States, stemming the blue flow of the Gulf Stream and into the face of rising seas rolling out of a tropical storm to our southeast. About a week had been allowed to make the transit and, with no port visits scheduled, a leisurely pace was set. We exercised at all battle, underway, damage control and condition stations, rigged for underway replenishment, towing, and helicopter refueling, went to abandon ship stations, updated our watch, quarter and station bills, inspected and became familiar with 5-inch gun emergency equipment, paraded the landing force, fired the two 5-inch guns and all our small arms, conducted man overboard drills, launched the whale boat, reviewed and practiced tactics and maneuvers, and conducted AAW tracking exercises with targets of opportunity (airliners). In short, we did as much as possible to prepare ourselves for the intensive eight-week course of training and tests we were to begin upon arrival at GITMO.

Within one hundred miles or so of the coast commercial radio may still be heard, especially in the evening with the bounce in full effect. During the transit south acid rock and the strains of Brahms could be heard topside mingling on the wind.

In the pilot house the quartermasters received Notice-To-Mariners, updated their charts, and plotted the position and intensity of the storm. Almost immediately upon getting underway one of the notices told us of a fishing boat, overdue from Jacksonville, FL by three days. With hundreds of thousands of commercial and pleasure boats from Maine to Mexico, notices like this are fairly common. The opportunity for finding this one, in the open sea, was very remote, but as an act of faith, the information was made part of the CO's night orders and all lookouts were briefed as they came on watch.

On the second day out, well off North Carolina, the weather deteriorated with the warm, wet wind rising above 35 knots and the seas marching in at ten to twelve feet. The ship rode well taking the swells nearly bow-on at a moderate speed. She pitched heavily, occasionally burying her nose, but the sickening, heavy rolls that normally accompany long-period storm waves was absent. Late in the afternoon a topside lookout reported a surface contact rising and falling in the seas. We maneuvered to intercept the contact, arriving just at dark. We had found the Jacksonville fishing boat!

She was adrift and slowly taking on water. Her engines were dead and there was no radio or electrical power for navigation lights. She was not in danger of swamping or capsizing, but rather, rode the long swells like a duck. The drag of her rudder and screw caused her to drift starboard quarter to the wind and seas. The boat was about 26 feet long, decked over forward, open aft with a low freeboard. A lightly built home-made roof extended aft from the windshield to provide relief from sun and rain. The cover of a single inboard engine rose up from the center of the open space aft. If it was rigged for overnight accommodations, they were not obvious. There were three men aboard. Despite their precarious circumstances, they seemed to be in good physical condition. With no power or lights, their immediate danger was of being run down by a ship surging north in the Gulf Stream.

We approached as closely as possible and, with loud hailer and hand signals, determined who they were and their condition. Darkness fell quickly in the overcast and our captain elected to steam circles around them all night rather than take a chance on losing one of them or one of our own in the pitch black sea. The boat had one operational hand flashlight aboard. With this fading light as our only aid in keeping contact, we went around and around throughout the night. We maintained a quarter- to a half-mile separation between the ship and boat, that being the practical limit of visibility.

Periodically the OODs tried to keep station on the boat to avoid crossing the seas and inducing gut-wrenching rolls, but it was impossible. The boat's drift speed was too slow to maintain steerageway and the wind blew the ship's head off into the troughs. I was concerned too that our presence would disturb the regular order of the waves causing the fishing boat to be swamped by breaking seas. It was a very uncomfortable night for all in the ship, but probably a great deal more so for the three in the boat.

Upon sighting the boat, we contacted the Coast Guard in Beaufort, NC by radio and Commander, Naval Surface Forces, US Atlantic Fleet in Norfolk, VA by formatted Navy message. We reported our position, the condition of the men and the boat and our intentions. The Coast Guard indicated they would dispatch a cutter to effect a rescue. It was to arrive at first light next morning.

I came on watch as the Officer of the Deck at 0400. The boat was so small and so near, and the seas were running so high that there was no radar return. We had to rely exclusively on eyes to maintain contact. The faint light on the boat was barely visible in the dark. About 0600 dawn broke faintly under heavily overcast skies. The wind had abated somewhat and the seas were regular, though still running high. We went around the boat several times, able to keep her in sight only with great difficulty. The long-sought light grew slowly dim. As the day brightened it washed out the boat's signal lamp. In the flat light of the dawn the boat disappeared! Four of us with binoculars could not pick her out of the sea. I reported the situation to the captain and maintained our circling, hoping, praying that she had not sunk. In about a half-hour the boat reappeared, standing clear of the waves and floating well, though obviously heavier than the previous evening. A great relief washed over me and the rest of the bridge watch.

Our Combat Information Center watch team had kept up an all-night running commentary with the Coast Guard and with COM-NAVSURFLANT. At first light the Coast Guard sent out a patrol aircraft which orbited the area but could not gain visual contact on us or the boat because of the low ceiling. The cutter, having gotten underway almost immediately upon receiving our report attempted to make headway through the seas but had to turn back sometime during the night because of wave damage. A larger replacement cutter from Norfolk would not be on scene for almost 24 hours. We were alone with the boat with no immediate help from the rescue and assistance experts.

When the light improved the CO thought we ought to close the boat to talk to them and re-affirm their condition. I directed my Junior Officer of the Deck (JOOD) to position the ship down wind and sea from the boat and make slow headway directly toward it. I intended to make an approach similar to that when recovering a man overboard. Point the ship directly at the target, pass it down one side or the other and effect recovery from the main deck. In this case we simply wanted to get close enough to talk. The closing rate was remarkably slow. We steered with rudder and engines. As we made our final approach, the ship rode up the face of a wave, and from inside the pilot house, the boat disappeared from view. Out on the starboard bridge wing the boat remained in sight. Though it would be close we could see the ship was not going to overrun the boat.

Without benefit of my view from the wing, the commanding officer, apparently thinking we were going to hit the boat, jumped out of his chair and ran around behind the control console in the center of the bridge. He pushed the helmsman off his station and *grabbed* the wheel. He swung it rapidly left and right several times but did not effectively change the direction of the ship. He also made a grab for the engine order telegraph but after a slight movement of one engine order handle, returned it to its original position. Wild eyed, he charged out onto the starboard bridge wing just in time to see the boat stabilized and riding easily along side about 10 yards distant. The boat rose and fell enormously in relation to the more stable destroyer. As the seas rolled beneath us, the boat was alternately in a hole down near the turn of the bilge, or above the main deck as it crested a wave.

The men were exhausted, wet and suffering from exposure. The boat continued to ship water making them bail more or less continually. They wanted to be taken aboard and let us know that in no uncertain terms. We were unprepared to remove them just then and if they had jumped into the sea there was a good chance we could not have recovered them. The wind and seas soon caused us to drift apart and we went back to circling, now with the benefit of full daylight.

About 0700 I was relieved as OOD. By then the executive officer was on the bridge. He, the CO and I (as Weapons Officer) conferred on the strategy to recover the men. I argued that that the men were deteriorating, the boat was sinking and we had to take them off. The thought of losing them again in the night was foremost in my mind. After much discussion the captain stated he was "prepared to go around them for the next 24 hours" while waiting for the Coast Guard cutter rather than take the risk of losing or injuring one of the fisherman in a rescue attempt. With that I spun about and stormed off the bridge down into the centerline passageway. Enroute I slammed the bridge door behind me. Instantly the 1MC barked, "Lieutenant Snyder, your presence is requested on the bridge." I returned to the bridge to face the wrath of the CO. He had strong words about my behavior, and then asked what I would do. "Remove them from the boat as soon as humanly possible," I instantly replied. Confronting the XO, he asked his opinion. The XO supported my position completely. The CO told the XO and me that we could do as we wished but it was our responsibility if something went wrong.

The plan was simple. We would make approaches similar to that earlier in the morning, sending over life jackets on the first pass and removing one man with each subsequent pass. Along with two gunner's mates with line throwing guns, I positioned a team of line handlers on the 01 level under the charge of the Chief Boatswain's Mate. Everyone was, of course, in life jackets. Three additional men were stationed on the main deck, in the shelter of the break, at the forward end of the superstructure. It was dangerous for them. The main deck was frequently waist deep in sea water. Each of them wore life jackets with life lines tended by two men from the 01 level.

On the bridge, I understand the XO took the conn, but I'm not certain. On the first approach the gunner fired over a projectile and shot line. The men towed over the three life jackets we had tied on. Originally intending to fire over the boat to give the men access to the shot line, I feared it would be blown or swept away. Instead I directed the gunner's mate to fire directly into the stern of the fishing boat. We shouted and signaled them to take cover, even passing the information on the topside speakers. They seemed not to comprehend or care. Propelled by a .45 caliber gas cartridge, the projectile, an air-filled, flexible plastic cylinder, ricocheted around inside the boat causing the men to shy away and duck for cover. The fishermen were very surprised at the power of the shot and velocity of the projectile. Fortunately we had the new soft projectiles. Earlier versions were brass bolts, about eight inches long. When the next whistle blew, indicating another shot was coming over, the boatmen immediately took cover.

On the second and subsequent passes we fired over a shot line attached to a manila messenger. One at a time, the men tied the messenger around themselves and jumped into the sea. The line handlers on the 01 level pulled them to the ship where the three men on the main deck, with the help of the boarding waves, assisted the fisherman aboard. The line handlers were a bit too enthusiastic with the first man, though. Rapidly hauled hand-over-hand, he spent a good bit of time underwater during the trip from the boat to the destroyer's side. The other two had an easier, slower transit, with the life jackets holding them face up in the water. Most dangerous was the period of time spent immediately along side the ship. Ships' sides are covered with projections for attaching ladders, nets, and boats, channeling water over the side, or pumping fluids from within. The waves, rising and falling more than ten feet, could easily rake the fisherman up and down the side. When the man in the water was hauled to the side, my three burly main deck seamen snatched him from the top of the wave. It instantly dropped away leaving the man suspended in mid air, to be unceremoniously dragged over the life lines. With help he scrambled up off his hands and knees, up the nearby inclined ladder and into the waiting arms of the corpsman and his assistants.

All three were brought aboard with relatively little damage. There were some line chafes and a few scrapes and bruises, but nothing was broken, and there were no tears or holes. We had all been lucky. The men were taken below, stripped of their wet things, showered, dried and put into donated clothing. They were fed, watered and given bunks in the chiefs' mess where they slept for the better part of twelve hours.

We reported our success to the Coast Guard and Navy and set course for Mayport, Florida, the Navy base at Jacksonville, leaving the fishing boat to fend for herself in the wild seas. Unfortunately, it contained all the gear necessary to conduct a small commercial line-fishing operation and the catch from a three day trip.

Enroute the three men volunteered to fish for red snapper, their original pursuit, to supplement the ship's general table fare. The seas were still running high restricting movement on the main deck. Their offer was courteously declined.

Two days after pulling the men from the Gulf Stream we arrived in Mayport to a grand reception. Navy and community officials, the fishermen's families, throngs of reporters, and well-wishers filled the pier. With mementos and memorabilia in hand, the three men left the ship to flashbulbs and applause. They were followed by our CO in a gleaming tropical white uniform. Alone, he held court on the pier answering questions and receiving the congratulations of the crowd. After a stay of several hours we got underway, resuming to our southbound course toward Cuba.

Several months later in Norfolk, after the ships return from refresher training, during a personnel inspection, I was surprised by a call to front-and-center. The CO presented me with the Navy Commendation Medal for my part in the Gulf Stream Rescue. From the day of the rescue to this, other than the words read from the citation, he never spoke of the incident, his behavior, or my part in the entire affair.

MAN OVERBOARD

BY DAVE HOOD

Graffiti commonly found on shitter walls onboard the *USS McKean (DD-784):*

"Another Frank Dumo memorial."

"God must love simple people. He made so many of them."

"What's a Humbert?"

When you get your car on the highway, your main purpose is to get from point A to point B. Oh sure — you may want to make a quick detour to see the world's largest non-stick frying pan or to drop by and visit your Aunt Jenny, but you don't want to distract too much from the original objective of getting to point B as rapidly and cheaply as possible.

When the US Navy puts one of its warships out in the sea lanes, its ultimate purpose may indeed be for it to go from, say, Seattle to San Diego. However, on the way there are certain obligations and exercises it is expected to participate in.

The *McKean* was homeported in Seattle but twice a year would transit to SoCal. As the crow flies (excuse me, I should say *as the seagull flies)* it's a one thousand, five hundred mile transit. At a cruising speed of twenty-five knots, the trip should take about sixty hours, or two and a half days. But the US Navy in general, and destroyers in specific, just don't do things that way. Have you ever walked your dog without a leash? Does he stay right on your heel and obediently keep pace with you? If he does he must have been trained by the United States Air Force. When I take my dog off of his leash, he dives into the bushes on the left side of the road and then leaps into the ditch on the right. He will pause to poop and then he will run as fast as he can to catch up and overtake me by a hundred yards. He will pee on a sign on the right side of the road and run back to me, only to stop and sniff a squashed snake on the left shoulder. For every yard I walk he must run twenty-five. That's what Navy destroyers do on a transit. They spend ten days on what could be a sixty-hour voyage.

Three or four times a day you have to go to "General Quarters, man all battle stations and set Material Condition Zebra throughout the ship" and keep doing it over and over until it can be done within five minutes or less.

And then you have to have a full power run just to see how fast this puppy can really go. And of course when you're doing thirty-six knots something just has to break. With any luck it won't be a lube pump or a flange but rather a bulkhead weld in the XO's cabin. So then you have to slow down and fix what you broke.

Then you have to drop a Mini Mobile Target (MMT) over the side and fire a *bird* (ASROC) and some *fish* (torpedoes) at it. And if there is not a Torpedo Retrieval Boat (TRB) you have to put a swimmer in the water and recover the exercise weapons that you just fired.

Then you're going to have to rendezvous with a bird farm and play life guard while the flattop launches and recovers aircraft.

And even though the ship has enough fuel to travel five thousand miles, you need to unrep at least every other day because you have burned up so much gas playing all of these silly games. And I can guarantee that on every late 1970s transit up and down the Pacific Coast of the US of A, we would pick up a sonar contact that would turn out to be a Soviet sub snooping around in the pond. If Ivan was in international waters we would stop everything we had been doing, set condition 1AS and follow him for as long as we could remain undetected. If he were in US territorial waters we would ping him to let him know that we found him and force him to run away.

Now spend a couple of days doing gunnery exercises (NGFS) destroying topsoil and feral goats on San Clemente Island or shooting at a target sled towed by either a tugboat or an aircraft (I should mention that we weren't actually encouraged to *hit* the sled. Sleds are expensive. An error degree was dialed into the synchros and we were expected to hit *near* the sled and *within* the error. This concept left all round-barrel gunner's mates spring-loaded to the torqued-off position and the good ones compensated for the error and did their best to actually blast the damn sled into itty-bitsy pieces of "Junk, Genuine, Expendable, Navy, unit of issue: send us more").

One final at-sea exercise that can kill a lot of time that could otherwise be expended on liberty in port is Man Overboard.

To do a man overboard drill, you need a dummy (remember that phrase; it plays a key part to this story). The dummy is traditionally named Oscar. Oscar is nothing more then a set of USN coveralls, stuffed with whatever, and wearing a kapok life preserver. Oscar would get tossed over the side and the ship would commence its man overboard drill.

There are several variations to man overboard. Let's say that Oscar and I are walking down the main deck and the ship goes into a trough and Oscar falls over the side. What's supposed to happen is that I grab the nearest life ring, toss it to Oscar and then report to the bridge that "Seaman Oscar just went overboard." The ship will turn around and then come in across the wind direction, with Oscar in its lee, so that the wind will tend to move the ship toward Oscar in the water, and not push him away, and the crew tries to snag Oscar (and the life ring) with a boat hook. Sometimes, it might be necessary to launch the motor whaleboat to recover Oscar.

If the After Lookout (or another crewman) should see someone fall over the side that will be reported to the bridge. While the ship is coming about, all hands will fall in for a muster so that the missing crewman can be rapidly identified (naturally, it will turn out to be Oscar but we're not supposed to know that until after the muster).

So there we are off the California coast. We could be in port. We could be on liberty. We could be drinking beer. We could be in a nudie bar. We could be drinking beer in a nudie bar while on liberty on solid land. But we're not going to do that. We're going to keep throwing a dummy over the side all day long.

I need to digress for a minute: We really did plan on pulling into San Diego eventually. The XO never liked us pulling into port with running rust or faded paint. He wanted to impress the other ships by showing how neat and clean and spiffy (I believe the *McKean*-term was sharp, shipshape and seamanlike) so the boatswain's mates were ordered to chase rust and paint as much of the ship as they possibly could, while underway and while still participating in all of these exercises.

Whenever the deck apes were off watch they were leaning over the side painting as much of the ship's hull that they could reach. Then someone would throw Oscar over the side and, *"This is a drill, this is a drill! Man overboard! Man overboard! Seaman Oscar has fallen overboard, port side!"* would be called. The deck apes would put down their brushes and rollers and run about the ship and recover the dummy. The word would be passed, *"Now secure from man overboard drill!"* and the boatswain's mates would discover that their paints have been knocked over and a gallon of Deck Gray has just spilled down the scuppers. They would break out some rags and thinner and lean over as far as they could when *"This is a drill, this is a drill, man overboard! Man overboard starboard side. All hands report to muster!"* Oscar would be hoisted aboard and the BMs would return to their painting only to discover that someone stepped in their pan of gray paint and left footprints all down the non-skid on the main deck. By the time they broke out some black paint to cover up the gray footprints *"This is a drill, this is a drill! Man overboard! Man overboard, port side! All hands report to muster!"*

Seaman Apprentice Humbert and the other deck apes on painting detail were getting awfully tired of this. They needed to figure out a way to end either the painting underway or the man overboard drills, or both. They put their heads together and came up with what they thought was a very good plan.

"Man overboard, man overboard! This is not a drill! Humbert fell overboard, port side! This is not a drill!"

"This is NOT a drill?"

"Who fell over the side?"

"This for real?"

"What's a Humbert?"

The ship came about and a very wet and three-quarters drowned Seaman Apprentice Humbert was plucked from over the side. His official story was that he was leaning over the side to do some painting when the ship rolled and he went over. He said that when the ship's wake went over him he really doubted if he would ever make it back to the surface.

The unofficial story is that if the other deck apes pitched in ten bucks each if he would be willing to go over the side "accidentally." They figured that a mishap might get the painting detail secured. Only half of the group paid him their share.

DANGEROUS LIAISONS

BY MIKE SNYDER

Destroyers refuel nearly every day when operating with carriers or in the company of a fleet oiler. Keeping the "tin cans" topped off is a neverending exercise. It was a hard-learned lesson of World War Two when a number of destroyers and their crews were lost after running out of fuel and being overwhelmed by wind and seas in a horrendous Pacific typhoon.

Underway replenishment is a difficult and dangerous evolution that brings ships very close together in all sorts of weather for hours at a time. There are many exciting and tragic stories of bumpings, collisions, emergency break-aways, parting lines, wires and hoses and near misses. They bubble to the top of conversation whenever destroyermen gather. Here is one from the other end of the fuel hose:

I was a GMT2 aboard the *USS Kitty Hawk* (CVA-63) on her first WestPac cruise in 1961. One of the first class petty officers in the division, GMT1 Phil Stewart, carried a large, disfiguring scar on his left arm. It was the result of a ship collision when his destroyer came too close to the carrier during unrep, rose up on a wave beneath an aircraft elevator and crushed the gun tub in which he was standing. In the *Kitty Hawk* my berthing space was well aft on the starboard side, just above the outboard screw. The skin of the ship was curved there as it transitioned from side to bottom with the water line about mid-way between our deck and overhead. You could easily hear the water slapping the hull through the steel plate.

Initially, underway replenishment was a reason to go up on deck. Experiencing the shiphandling and the seamanship was exciting, even exotic. At high speed, the destroyers ran up alongside, plunging and leaping as the fuel harnesses were passed. Standing waves developing between the ships crashed aboard. On deck, men tended the phone and distance line while the refueling rig crews strained against wire rope and ungainly six-inch rubber hose. Heavy spray often raked the entire ship while an occasional green sea would inundate the fo'c'sle causing seamen to duck behind machinery and shields and hang on. Active sonar pulsed and screeched through the water setting your teeth on edge. At night the drama was amplified with a multitude of colored lights indicating distance between the ships, showing hose and wire catenary, directing in- and out-haul commands, transmitting messages, and revealing the movements of the men to whom they were pinned. The thrill decreased to ho-hum, though, as the fiftieth and hundredth unrep was completed. Eventually, even the night unreps weren't enough to rouse me out on deck.

In my berthing space was a sounding tube used to gauge a deep jet-fuel tank. As the carrier took aboard oceans of fuel the sounding watchman climbed in and out of our compartment all night dropping his spanner wrench and rattling the weighted tape up and down the sounding tube. Early one morning I woke to someone shaking me and a voice forcefully saying, "Get Up! Don't light lights or matches!" The acrid odor of JP-5 was overwhelming. We were taking fuel from a tanker that night. When our tank was pressed-up (filled to the top), it had overflowed through the carelessly left-open sounding tube, flooding the space to a depth of several inches. My twenty ship-mates and I quickly made our way up to the damage control deck, then over into our workspaces, the aft special weapons magazines. It was several days before we could re-occupy the berthing space and the odor didn't completely go away until we scaled-up the tile to clean the deck beneath.

When destroyers were alongside refueling, they pinged their active sonar incessantly. Later, as a Weapons Department officer I learned that was unnecessary because the noise of unrep rendered them virtually useless, but in the 1960s it must have been fleet policy. It was nerve-wracking. The sound transmitted through the water directly into my berthing space when a tin can was alongside. The high-pitched squeal resonated in the compartment making sleep nearly impossible.

It took a while, but as I listened to the old hands tell collision stories and saw Phil Stewart's wrecked arm, watched the destroyers leaping and careening close alongside, heard their sonar shrieking near the pain threshold, and awakened at 0300 to a potential bomb in my berthing compartment, it began to dawn on me that my living space, my home away from home, might not actually be the safest place for me. Eventually, when an increase in the deafening sonar signals announced a destroyer's approach I migrated out of the berthing space to the relative safety and comfort of the air-conditioned storerooms and offices of the SASS (Special Aircraft Service Stores, AKA nuclear weapons) spaces. Down there it was quiet, clean, cool, and free of sounding tubes. It became a way of life; not completely approved by our officers, but not stopped by them either. Until leaving the *Kitty Hawk* in the Philippines in December, 1961 I regularly took myself away from the hazards of seagoing dangerous liaisons and slept in the ammunition magazines.

MIDWATCH

BY ROBIN SMITH

After a week at sea, fatigue made sleep come easy. I would sometimes be asleep before my head hit the pillow, and dreams would soon follow. The dreams were typical of a hedonistic young sailor, from past ports of call to home and the girl I left behind. Every now and then, my dreams would be rudely interrupted. "Smitty!" a voice would call. In my dreams I would stop and look for the source of this voice, which came in whispers, and seemingly far away.

"Smitty!" the voice would call again. The dreamscape would quake, and then fade to black. Consciousness would begin to return slowly, and my eyes would open. I often awoke to see a shadow cast on the partition of my cubicle by a halo of red light. I would roll onto my back, and turn my head toward the suspected source. The red light was bright, and from a small source. "Smitty, it's 2330. You've got the midwatch," a voice from beyond the light would tell me. "Wha … uh … oh, yeah, Okay! I'm up!" was my response. The light fell to the floor illuminating a circle on the deck, and revealing a pair of boondockers in need of a spit shine, and the hem of worn bell-bottomed blue jeans. There's no place for modesty on board ship, and in a compartment of 66 other men. I slept on the lower rack in a stack of three. I pulled back the covers, laying there in my skivvies, and rolled out of my rack and onto my feet in a smooth motion that would have impressed an Olympic gymnast. The evil wrecker of my dreams spun around on his heels and departed, leaving me there to dress in the dark.

I grabbed my socks, and pushed my feet into them. I worked my way upward until I was finally dressed. I grabbed my ball cap and placed it on my head as I made my way to the starboard fire door, my eyes still heavy with sleep. I walked into the ladder well, which was lit with red light. I climbed through the hatch opening onto the second deck. Operations' berthing was situated on the third deck, and engineering on the second. A pair of 180s and I was on another ladder to the main deck. The large, heavy hatches were *Zebra* fittings, and were propped open at a 45 degree angle. They were only closed when the ship was at battle stations, or other conditions requiring watertight integrity.

The hatches were obstacles for a tall sailor. Small scuttle

hatches in their center had dog wheels that protruded downward, and upward. This small, circular hatch allowed quick access into a space when the main hatch was closed. The wheels could raise a nasty lump, or cut the scalp of the unwary sailor. I always climbed in a stoop to avoid such unpleasantries.

Another set of 180s and I was on the main deck, and began my way forward. On the *Spruance*-class destroyers the berthing spaces for Supply, Engineering and Ops were stacked from the main deck down, with the helo deck topping the stack. Supply was on the main deck. Only the aft portion of the main deck, the fantail, was exposed to the elements. Two passageways ran the length of the ship on port and starboard sides up to the rope locker at the bow. I stepped through a watertight door and passed main engine room number two. The soft whine of the gas turbines could be heard issuing from below.

I stepped through an archway, and to my left was a passageway that ran athwartships, leading to the galley and enlisted mess. I had to wince as I made my way over to the port side, and the serving line, due to the white light. The light destroyed my night vision, but I wanted to see what the mess cooks had whipped up for midrats.

Midrats, or midnight rations, were served to sailors coming off watch, or going on watch at midnight. Some sailors would forgo the evening meal and try to catch some sleep before they stood their watches late in the evening, or early in the morning. The meal was normally a light one, and tonight they were serving my favorite dish: beanie-weenies! There is no finer culinary delight than baked beans and chopped up frankfurters. I wasn't terribly hungry, but I grabbed a tray anyway and stepped up to the service line. The cook drove his serving spoon into a steeping pan of beanie-weenies and dolloped a heaping serving onto my tray. I walked on to the cookie tray and found chocolate chip cookies on tap for desert. Life doesn't get any better. I took two, but then covering one hand with the tray, I tried to steal a third. From out of nowhere a set of tongs flew through the air and hit my hand. With a mild yelp I pulled my hand back. A Filipino cook stared back at me with menace in his eyes, so I didn't push my luck any further. Those Filipino cooks worked those tongs like Bruce Lee worked a pair of nunchucks. They were dangerous. I gave an impish grin and moved on.

I walked to the enlisted mess and selected a table. Putting my tray down I grabbed a glass and poured myself a glass of milk. I didn't have much time, so I had to wolf down the tasty repast sitting before me. Chugging my milk, grabbing my cookies and tray, I made my way to the scullery. My tummy was full, and I was one happy sailor as I made my way back to the starboard side, and the red-lit passageway.

I passed through another archway and watertight door and turned into another athwartships passageway. The ship was narrower here, and the passageway wasn't as long. I walked past the ship's gedunk and store and stepped up to the centerline ladder, which took me to the O-1 level.

Taking a 180 turn I stood behind the ship's computer center, then executed another 180 to take the ladder up to the O-2 level. The ship's Combat Information Center (CIC) was on the O-2 level. I had one more deck to go, and another pair of 180s, up another ladder and I was almost there. A 180 and a dogleg took me past the bridge's head, and the skipper's sea cabin. Now, I was in complete darkness. I put my arms out to feel for bulkheads, and the watertight door at the end of the passageway. My night vision was gone and what little ambient light there was was inadequate for me to see. I passed the charthouse, whose watertight door was shut. A few more steps and I stood at the watertight door that opened onto the bridge. The door was dogged down, so I groped for the dog handle. Lifting it disengaged the dogs, and allowed the door to swing freely into the bridge.

Immediately, I was greeted with the din of a dozen men speaking all at once. The changing of the watch was in full swing. As I entered, to my left stood the CIC phone talker and his relief. They were discussing the contacts being tracked by CIC. The board was composed of a Lucite plate, illuminated through the sides, with information written in a colored grease pencil that would glow from the light. The board showed four active contacts, with the last one designated *T* (tango). It had been a busy day. Immediately in front of me was an NTDS (Naval Tactical Data System) display. It was a huge console with an amber-colored radar screen, which was flanked by amber lit buttons. I gingerly made my way to the port side where the Quartermaster's station was. To get there I had to negotiate an obstacle course of consoles and bodies. The helm was crowded with watchstanders, and the officers stood at the front of the bridge. I squeezed myself between the helm console and the magnetic compass binnacle. The quartermaster of the watch greeted me, "Hey Smitty, how're ya doin'?"

"Finer'n frog hair! Wha's up?"

My striker launched into his spiel detailing the status of the engineering plant, course, speed, problems encountered, the captain's night orders, and the navigator's night orders. I paid careful attention taking detailed mental notes. I was going to have to write this all down in the first log entry of the day. Then we turned our attention to the chart table. He turned on the red light over the table, and we leaned down on our elbows to look at the navigation problem I was facing. It was simple: a rectangular track was laid out, which we were to follow until well after I was relieved. The QMOW pointed out our current position, the time to the next turn, and the new course and speed. The winds were light, and we were inside the Gulf Stream, so we shouldn't expect any significant drift. We were immediately joined by the offgoing and oncoming Officers and Junior Officers of the Deck (OOD and JOOD). The six of us must have looked like a football team in a huddle as we sized up the situation. As the minutes ticked off, the oncoming watch standers requested permission to relieve their counterparts. The OOD acknowledged each, and instructed the relieved watchstanders to strike below. With each relief, the bridge grew quieter.

As if on cue the six of us broke up and went to our next station. Satisfied I understood the orders of the evening, and all conditions affecting my post, I informed my striker I was ready to relieve him.

"Officer of the deck, Petty Officer Smith, I am ready to assume duties as Quartermaster of the watch!"

"Officer of the deck, aye!"

"Officer of the deck, Seaman Schmuck, I stand relieved!"

"Officer of the deck, aye! Strike below!"

"Aye, sir!"

"Alright Smitty, I had it; you got it; don't break it! I'll see you in a few hours."

As soon as the OOD and JOOD were relieved, the change of the watch was complete and the bridge grew quiet. But, I had to get busy; there were things to do.

I turned first to the log table and opened the logbook to a new page. At the top, far left, I entered the date, and time 0000. I wrote down the status of the engineering plant, special orders, and the names of my fellow watch standers. Anything that might have any legal implications should the ship run into trouble was noted in the log. Once that was completed, I turned back to the chart to double check our current dead-reckoning position and the predicted time to turn. I turned out the light then proceeded to do my weather report.

Every six hours, ships at sea are required to send a weather report to Norfolk (on the Atlantic coast). Temperature, true winds, relative humidity, cloud type and altitude, snow/rain/sleet/thunder, sea state, and other data are recorded then assembled into a formatted radio message. At midnight some of these things are hard to determine, especially if there is no moon, and blank codes go into the message for the unavailable data. This takes several minutes and requires visits to a couple of stations on the bridge to gather the data. Wind gauges on the bridge gave you relative wind direction and speed, then you had to use a maneuvering board (*mo-board*) to determine true wind speed and direction. I didn't know it at the time, but this was my first introduction to vector algebra. The radio message was put into a thin can, then inserted into a pneumatic tube and sent to the radio room.

With that out of the way, I would read the skipper's night orders. Go to the chart room, and perform the sacred ritual of all quartermasters who are assigned to ships: the daily winding and calibrating of the ship's chronometers.

Each ship had three chronometers. There were extremely precise clocks, each about the size of melon, and weighing several pounds. They were made of brass and non-ferrous metals. The ship's crew would use the three clocks in the event they had to abandon ship. One clock went into the CO's launch, another with the whaleboat, and the third with a QM assigned to a raft. A QM in each group would use a clock for navigating. In my opinion they were worthless, especially considering that there was only one copy of the publications needed to perform celestial navigation calculations. But, woe unto any QM who let his clocks run down. It was a serious matter, and pains were taken to ensure these clocks kept ticking. It was, therefore, a daily ritual to wind the clocks as soon as possible on the midwatch. Once they were wound, their time was compared to the timing broadcast of WWV out of Boulder, CO, where atomic clocks kept time. The deviations from the clocks' time to the atomic time were recorded in the appropriate log, and they too, would accompany their respective clock to its place in the boats, and rafts. They would be used to calculate the time-drift of the clocks so corrections could be made to the times in the absence of the atomic time broadcast.

The next item was to check the satellite receiver for the latest fix. Since the constellation of navigation satellites didn't offer global coverage 24/7, fixes weren't obtained with any regularity. If a fix was ready, it was plotted on the chart, and all dead reckoning positions and times were updated accordingly.

Weather reports were also received regularly, and the weather chart had to be updated. By the time all of these tasks were completed an hour had passed, and only then would things begin to get real slow!

It was now close to 0100 local time before the QMOW of the midwatch had a chance to relax. The midwatches were normally quiet. Rarely were there any training exercises scheduled for this time of night. The crew was tired enough, and it didn't make much sense to rob them of badly needed sleep for training that could be done during more reasonable hours. So, for the next couple of hours this night our job was to keep the ship inside a box, sailing east for some time, then turning north, west, south and back east again. Not terribly taxing. Once things had settled down, the QMOW was free to mosey about the bridge and contemplate the universe, or whatever was on his mind, just as long as he was on time notifying the OOD of changes in course and speed.

I enjoyed stargazing during the midwatch. I spent my teens in rural Wisconsin, and was no stranger to the night sky. However, I never truly saw the night sky until I was out in the middle of the ocean. The night sky at sea was so dark that even colors of the stars could be discerned. Various nebulae, the Milky Way, and the Andromeda Galaxy were easily visible when the moon wasn't up. Truly magnificent!

When I had my fill of the night sky, the ocean itself was a source of wonder. In warmer waters the phytoplankton, diatoms, and other bioluminescent creatures would glow green in our wake. From time to time some would shine exceptionally brightly, and would sparkle like micro-novae in the glowing foam. The pressure change caused by the passing of our wake would cause the critters to glow. In one spectacular instance, our sonar crew was working the sonar late at night. We were off the coast of Africa and the waters were very warm, and very full of these *glow in the dark* creatures. The ping jockeys emitted a single pulse from the sonar dome, which was immediately visible as a thin, green circle traveling at the speed of sound in water. It seemed to take only an instant to travel to the horizon, which was eight nautical miles away as viewed from the bridge of the *Spruance*.

These spectacles were at their best during moonless nights. With a full moon, the stars and the seas were simply boring. When I was bored, and tired of standing, I would wedge myself between the log table and some electrical boxes which jutted out from the aft bulkhead. It was a precarious perch, and not necessarily as comfortable as a chair, but it worked for a little while. On this perch I could swap sea stories with the boatswain's mate of the watch. Only being on my first tour of duty, my sea stories were few, and not always very entertaining. Consequently, I was usually the audience for Boats.

No two midwatches were ever the same. On one midwatch, the moon hung low on the horizon and gave the scene an eerie look. The image was made even more eerie when the OOD turned on the hydrophone speakers on the bridge. Suddenly, the bridge was filled with groans, creaks, whistles and clicks of various volumes and pitches. I almost expected a monster to rise up out of the sea and try to take us under (too many Japanese B-movies!). These sounds were fascinating. One noise caught my attention, and the OOD told me it was a carpenter fish. I had never heard of such a thing, and he explained that it was actually a sperm whale echo-locating its next meal. It emitted sound pulses that sounded like someone pounding nails. As the whale neared its prey, the pulses came closer and closer in time then would suddenly stop. The prey had been caught.

Most midwatches were pretty boring, and for some with the duty it became a chore just to stay awake. I was not a fan of Navy coffee, particularly after observing the destructive effects coffee had on the wax coating of the bridge deck, and watching a chief use it as an effective solvent.

On one rare instance a midwatch became very exciting. In December of 1977, we had taken part in NATO exercises, and made three liberty stops in Europe. After all was said and done, the US components of the exercise were freed to steam independently back home. After leaving the Baltic, we had to transit the North Sea and the English Channel to get home. The North Atlantic was unusually calm, given its reputation. The midwatch during this transit was as boring as it could get. I was wedged into my perch waiting for something that needed my attention. I did not have to wait long.

There was no moon this night, but I became aware of a light source permeating the bridge. Its spectral characteristics indicated a man-made source. I waited a few minutes to see if any reports came to the bridge, and to make sure I was certain of what I was seeing. When no one responded to this situation, I began to investigate. I walked to the starboard bridge wing, and as I crossed the bridge I noted that the horizon was barely visible. Peering out the starboard side, I saw nothing. I went to the port bridge wing, and there the source was: A cruise ship!

"Officer of the Deck, I have a surface contact off the port quarter, aspect angle 350 degrees crossing our fantail headed to port. Distance approximately four nautical miles!"

"Wha …" The OOD arrived at the port bridge wing door before the "…t?" got there. The ship was lit up like the Las Vegas strip. It had created a false dawn at zero dark 30. The OOD sped back to the centerline gyro repeater, and grabbed the bitch box receiver. He called up CIC and raised three kinds of hell. The JOOD in the meantime was now on the bridge wing trying to take in the source of light that was now casting visible shadows in our bridge. Now the OOD was reading the riot act to the lookouts on the signal bridge and fantail. You would have thought I kicked over a hornet's nest. The CIC phone talker was jabbering away demanding info from his counterpart in the compartment right below him. Meanwhile, I strode back to my perch and made the appropriate logbook entries. I don't recall hearing a single yawn for the remainder of the watch.

At 0345 the relief process begins anew as the morning watch arrives for their duty. I would return to my bunk, and would be instantly asleep. Reveille would arrive all too soon.

DOG ZEBRA

BY DAVE HOOD

During underway replenishments my assignment was ship-to-ship phonetalker. Linehandlers on the main deck, some six feet above the waterline, were always wet and cold, no matter how calm the seas were. The ship-to-ship phonetalker stood on the flightdeck on the O-1 level, got to see everything, stayed dry and got the opportunity to shoot the breeze with his counterpart on the other ship.

If you're a destroyer sailor, you're familiar with an unrep. If you're not, let me explain the process. Ships at sea burn a lot of fuel. I heard that the typical fuel consumption was one hundred gallons per hour? Destroyers may get their best fuel economy at, say fifteen knots. At that speed, a FRAM has a range of five thousand eight hundred miles. But remember - this is a destroyer story, written by a destroyer sailor to be read by other destroyer sailors who have all served aboard destroyers. And what is it that destroyers like to do best? We like to go real fast. And the only thing that consumes more fuel then a destroyer with all of its boilers lit off is the space shuttle on take-off.

About every three days we would need to top off. The *heavy* could be a fleet oiler such as the *USNS Cayuga*, a replenishment ship such as the *USS Mount Shasta (AE-33)* or even an aircraft carrier. The escort would pull up alongside the heavy and try to maintain a constant distance of about one hundred and twenty feet apart and a constant speed of about twelve knots. A shot-line would be fired from one ship to the other. Attached to the projectile was a spool of common "550" parachute cord, orange in color. The heavy would attach a heavier line to their end of the shot-line. The escort's line-handlers would haul the shot-line back aboard. Then the heavier line would be pulled aboard. To the heavier line, they would attach an even heavier line. Spliced onto that line would also be the sound-powered phone line. The phone-talker (me) would plug in and be able to speak directly to his counterpart on the other ship. That heavier line would be pulled aboard by the line-handlers. Finally, they would attach a steel cable to the end of the line and that would be pulled aboard the escort. The cable would be attached to a fitting on the escort's fueling station.

The fuel probe would slide down the cable and mate up with the fuel station. The ships would then steam side by side for as long as it took to transfer fuel. It usually took about an hour. It always seemed to take longer if the weather was crappy.

On a FRAM, we traditionally used the fueling station on the flight deck at the rear of the ship — located forward of the rear 5-inch gun mount. There was another fueling station forward, up on the torpedo deck, just forward of the bridge. For some unknown reason, we rarely used this station at sea.

One night off the California coast we pulled up alongside the aircraft carrier *USS Kitty Hawk (CVA-63)*. As soon as our communications were established I told my counterpart that we were requesting forty thousand gallons of DFM and that the maximum pressure that we could receive was 100-psi.

"Wait one," came the response.

"McKean, Kitty Hawk. The minimum pressure that we can send is one hundred and twenty psi."

"Wait one." It was my turn to use the standard Navy response phrase. I told that to the engineering representative and he told me that it shouldn't be a problem.

"Kitty Hawk, McKean. We are standing by to receive forty-thousand gallons of DFM at one hundred and twenty psi minimum."

"Roger that, McKean. Forty thousand at one hundred and twenty psi minimum."

Did you notice that I started the preceding paragraph by saying, "One night?" That's right. Night. As in dark. Real dark. Middle of the freakin' ocean dark. One thing about US Navy warships at sea at night: they don't like to show lights. Pure darkness is the rule. The only topside illumination comes from special floodlights that have red lenses. They project just enough light for you to see what you're doing but not much more than that.

So there we were. It was the middle of the night in the middle of the ocean. Two ships tethered together steaming at twelve knots. My ship weighed two thousand, two hundred and fifty tons, the other weighed eighty-six thousand tons. We were three hundred and ninety feet long and forty feet wide. The *Kitty Hawk* was one thousand and sixty-nine feet long and two hundred and fifty-two feet wide. Our main deck was six feet above the waterline. The *Kitty Hawk's* flight deck was eighty-five feet above the waterline. They had the gas and we needed it. Everything was equitable.

After awhile the engineering rep told me to tell the *Kitty Hawk* that our tanks were nearly full and for them to prepare to cease pumping.

"Kitty Hawk, McKean. Standby to cease pumping."

"Kitty Hawk aye. Standing by."

Five minutes later, and I was instructed to pass on the word to cease pumping. I was instructed that we would want a back-suction and *then* a blow-down." The ship-to-ship fueling hose is corrugated rubber and about five inches in diameter and several hundred feet long. It must hold hundreds of gallons of fuel. A 'back-suction' is supposed to suck the fuel out of the hose and back in to the tanker's fuel tanks. A 'blow-down' is the forcing of compressed air through the hose to blow any vapors into the receiving ship's fuel tanks.

"McKean, Kitty Hawk. Standby for your back-suction and blow-down."

"McKean aye. Standing by."

There are no instruments nor are there any gauges on the flight deck. Nothing to indicate what is happening. But I could tell something wasn't right. Instead of the sucking, wheezing sound of fuel being sucked out of the fuel hose, I heard something different, something unfamiliar. Before I could figure out what was different I heard the new sound of popping metal and expanding gases. I could now no longer see the fuel probe. It was swallowed up in a fog. The fog then expanded forward towards me. That didn't make any sense! We were moving forward at twelve knots and yet the fog was coming up from behind and catching up with us. And then the fog swallowed up me. It was wet and it smelled. It clung to me and penetrated my clothing. It was fuel! I realized what happened. Instead of giving us a *back-suction* and sucking out all of the remaining fuel in the hose, the *Kitty Hawk* started off with a *blow-down*. The remaining fuel was being forced into our already-full tanks. The high-pressure air driving the fuel was atomizing it and the fueling station's seals blew under the pressure. The entire aft end of the ship was enveloped in an expanding cloud of fuel!

I could feel the fuel penetrating my clothing and clinging to my skin. *"Cease pumping! Cease pumping! Cease pumping! Kitty Hawk, McKean! Stop your goddamn pumping!"* I again looked at this cloud of fuel that had swallowed us up. I began to envision someone coming out on deck: someone ignoring the fact that the smoking lamp was out. I looked at the fuel fog that swallowed up the red lens flood lights. I wondered about the condition of the waterproof gaskets. I just knew that at any moment the vapors would ignite. Would I be aware of the flash? Would it instantly sear me? Would I have time to see it ignite and then envelope me?

I took off my helmet and let it fall to the deck. I took the sound-powered phone set off of my head. I was about to discard that too and then run. But run where? I'm on a ship in the middle of the ocean. There was nowhere to run to. It wouldn't matter where I ran to. If the ship exploded I would be just as dead on the bow as I would on the flight deck. And if I was to die I might as well die on my station doing my duty.

I put the phones and helmet back on. By then the *Kitty Hawk* must have realized their error for they were now giving us our back suction. By the time that was done the wind blowing over the ship had dissipated the fuel fog. The *Kitty Hawk* retracted the fuel probe and I disconnected the phone set and tossed their phone line over the side. I don't recall if I sealed the jack in a plastic bag or not. We released the pelican hook and let the cable go. We maneuvered to starboard and got some distance between us and the *Kitty Hawk* and then returned to our lifeguard station in her wake. All of us on the aft station were hosed off with a 1-½" fire hose and then excused from water hours so we could take a hot fresh water shower.

Two days later we again refueled from the *Kitty Hawk*.

UNREP

BY ROBIN SMITH

Endurance, this is the key to projection of power, and protection of national interests half a world away. There's little you can do in this regard if your ships lack the ability to get to, and operate in, distant battle zones. You can't go searching for a friendly port when you need fuel, food, or ammo. To solve this problem, the Navy has created a fleet of auxiliary vessels capable of keeping our ships gassed up, armed, and the crews fed. This also includes precious mail from loved ones back home.

Underway Replenishment is a simple evolution in appearances. A supply vessel steams a steady course and speed, while one or two ships steam alongside taking on supplies, oil, or transferring personnel and mail. The supply vessels may be oilers, reefers, or even carriers. The modern oilers (AOE — Auxiliary Oil and Explosives) can carry the fuel and ammo to keep a fleet in action. They even carry a limited supply of foodstuffs. Reefer ships (AFs) carry the bulk of the foodstuffs. Carriers also can provide fuel oil to other ships in the battle group if the need arises. While unrep is simple in principle, it can be a very exhaustive effort, and is fraught with dangers.

The process begins when the battle group turns into the sea and the ships in need of supply take stations astern and to the sides of the supply ship. The supply ship flies the *Romeo* flag from the yard-arms at half-staff indicating the ship is not yet ready. When all participants are ready, the supply ship *two-blocks* (flies at full staff) Romeo, and the first ships go to full speed to pull alongside. The ships pull alongside at a distance of one hundred and eighty feet optimally, more in rough seas. Once the ships have matched speed and course with the supply ship, a gunner's mate fires a small missile across, which carries a rope the other crew retrieves. This rope is hooked to a cable that will act as the transfer support line. Supplies and fuel lines are then passed back along these cables. One cable is not used for transfers, but carries small pennants and markers. These are for the officer of the deck (OOD), whose job is to make sure the distance between ships remains constant. There is some room for deviation, but not much.

The crews involved with the re-supply are wearing bulky life vests and helmets, all colored orange for visibility. They scurry about their stations making connections and moving supplies about for storage, and to make room for more. It's a hard, dirty and dangerous job. The pallets swing as the ships rock to and fro. They may hit unwary sailors inflicting injury. The cables may break if the ship's distance is not properly maintained, or the ships sway to extremes in heavy seas. The broken cables, under high tension, can inflict serious injury on the topside crewmembers.

The weather and seas show no mercy either. The air may be already cold, but spray from the waves makes it worse. Even in calm seas, the bow wakes from both ships bounce off each other's hulls. Where trough meets trough the water creates deep bowls, and where crest meets crest, the result can be a tower of water that breaks against the side of the ships. Getting wet seems a minor problem when one considers the possibility of being washed overboard. In heavy seas, the problems associated with the turbulent waters between the ships are amplified! As a safeguard, helicopters are airborne, and ships in trail standby to assist anyone who goes for an unexpected swim.

Unrep involves most of the crew, particularly on the smaller ships. Once supplies are set down, they must be moved aside, and then taken below. The supplies are passed through hatches, doors, or by elevator. The deck is alive with activity, but things are happening on the ship's bridge as well.

What goes on on the bridge of a ship during unrep looks calm, but tensions are high. The OOD is constantly monitoring the guideline and issuing minor course and speed changes as necessary. Looking over his shoulder are other officers (who are learning as they watch) as are the XO and CO, who are making sure the OOD doesn't scratch the paint job of either ship. All this transpires on the bridge wing, while inside the helmsman and lee helmsman respond to issued orders.

Steering a ship is not a difficult chore, especially in mirror-smooth seas. It gets a little more challenging as the sea state degrades. Nonetheless, there are some evolutions that require an expert hand, and unrep is one of these situations. Unrep is reserved for one of the ship's master helmsmen who is a member of the ship's quartermaster gang. Working in concert with the OOD their work ensures the safety of ship and crew while the ship is re-supplied underway. As a 20-year-old quartermaster seaman, I was one of the first of the junior sailors to qualify as the *Spruance's* master helmsman. To achieve this distinction, I had to master the helm during unrep.

The memory of my first time alongside is clouded with the passage of time. I can't remember the name of the supply ship, or the other ships involved, when or where. All I remember is the ships were haze gray and underway. I was excited at the chance to prove my mettle. I wasn't nervous at all; I was ready! As the ship made preparations, our CO, Commander Raymond Harbrecht, called me over to his chair on the starboard side of the bridge. Like a father he gave me counsel on what was expected of me, and how best to perform my duties. Shortly thereafter I relieved the helm, and we got ourselves ready for unrep.

Since this was my first time alongside, everyone was informed that we would not make connections when we got into position. We would sail in formation for several minutes — until everyone was confident I could do the job — then go around and do it for real. The seas weren't very heavy, but weren't smooth either. I watched the compass card on the gyro repeater on the console before me. Occasionally, I would glance up to see how things were going, but seldom, and only short glances. I noted that Romeo was at half-staff telling us to wait. Meanwhile, I concentrated and kept my ship on course. I hate to get "Zen" about the whole ordeal, but I did become "one" with my ship. It was the OOD, the compass card, the ship's wheel, and me. Everything else faded from consciousness as I performed my job.

That was until I found us alongside the supply ship. A CH-46 Sea Knight helicopter was running up her engines on her flight deck, and the sound grew louder as we steamed up alongside. I had not heard the command to the lee helm to punch it! My excitement grew, but I didn't panic. My heart raced; my palms sweated; and my muscles tensed. The course changes came periodically.

"Come left, steer zero-niner-zero point five!"

"Come left, steer zero-niner-zero point five, Aye! ... Steering zero-niner-zero point five!"

"Very well!"

This exchange between the OOD and me was followed shortly by,

"Come right, steer zero-niner-one!"

"Come right, zero-niner-one, Aye! ... Steering zero-niner-one!"

"Very well."

As we settled in alongside the supply ship the course and

speed changes became fewer and further between.

Time was standing still, and I had no idea how long we were alongside. Suddenly, "All ahead flank! Steady as she goes!" was shouted to the lee helm and me. The *Spruance* sprinted out ahead of the supply ship, then, "Hard right rudder!"

"Hard right rudder, Aye!"

The *Spruance* heeled over to port. I gave my reports according to procedure:

"My rudder is hard right, passing one-zero-zero!"

"Very well! Belay your headings!"

"Belay my headings, Aye!"

Just like that, it was over. After completing the turn, I was immediately relieved of the helm. My hands were soaked in sweat and I rubbed them on my pants. The officers praised my performance, and I was given a chance to relax before we got in position for the real thing. I had a smile on my face that would have impressed the Cheshire cat. I was ecstatic, excited and proud that I had done what was expected of me, and did it well. I did complain about not being informed we were going alongside. Not that it ultimately mattered, but it removed the element of surprise.

When we took up stations again, I relieved the helm once more. This was the real deal, and this time the OOD made sure I was aware we were going alongside. The lines were passed, and the necessary supplies transferred. When the transfer was completed, the lines were released, and hauled back aboard.

As before the order for flank speed was issued, but unlike before, I was given my first introduction to a tradition: The *break-away song*. As the *Spruance* darted out ahead of the supply ship, the lilting tones and guitar riffs of John Denver's "Leaving On a Jet Plane" issued from the ship's loudspeaker system. I'm a Denver fan, and I like that song a lot, but the *Spruance* was a man o'war, a ship of the line, and "Leaving On a Jet Plane" lacked a certain... machismo. I was mortified! I was informed that this was the CO's selection. He too appreciated John Denver's music, and thought this song befitting since the *Spruance* was the Navy's first gas-turbine ship. Yeah, we did sound like a DC-10 running up for take-off, but still...

Unrep soon became routine, but I was eventually presented with a bigger challenge. On this occasion, the seas were rough. The waves striking the bow caused a yaw of several degrees. We went in, and got to work. This time, however, it was me against the sea. One quick glance out the port door to the bridge wing revealed waves washing over the gunwales of the oiler. I thought to myself, "God, I feel bad for those guys out there!" I was busting my butt trying to keep the ship steady in heavy seas. It was impossible to keep the ship on course. Still, the OOD was issuing half-degree course changes. I laughed to myself, and thought, "Yeah, right!" The best I could do was to make sure the average heading was on the course specified. If memory serves, this was one of those rare instances when a dose of medicinal brandy was given to those who worked topside. After I was relieved, I could have used a good belt myself!

THE COFFEE POT

BY TERRY MILLER

The *Houston Chronicle's* Leon Hale, a favorite humor columnist, once wrote of making instant coffee because he doesn't like to wash the coffee pot. As a student working in the University of Oklahoma's Animal House (actually, it was where small animals involved in biological research were housed, not where the fraternity guys lived) I worked for a professor of microbiology who never washed his coffee cup. I think it's time to own up to something that many of us do where I work. We don't wash them, either. We just keep using them.

I have always been something of a coffee hound and while a field manager for Western Union, kept a cup at each of the offices in my area of responsibility. Since I only visited those cities once a month or so, and since I don't use cream or sugar in my coffee, any germs on those cups would long since have died of starvation, wouldn't they? (If I'm wrong, don't tell me. I'd rather not know.)

How many other people drink coffee at work? Probably at least half of them, wouldn't you say? How many of them wash their cups after the last swallow? I don't mean sloshing a little water around in it, I mean washing it. Yeah, that's what I think, too. So rinsing it and wiping it out with a paper towel once in a while is probably more the norm than actually washing it, isn't it? I've even known some people who swore soap or detergent left a funny taste in the cup or pot.

When I was in the Navy I was assigned to Sonar Control

where a thirty-cup urn provided hot coffee twenty-four hours a day, made fresh every four hours. It was never washed. Oh, it was rinsed out each time when the junior man on duty would carry it down four decks and from just aft of CIC and the bridge to the aft crew's head where the only sink deep enough to accommodate the large pot was located. The basket of coffee grounds would be emptied over the side along the route and the whole thing would then be rinsed, refilled, and carried back up to sonar control so that fresh coffee was ready for the men coming on for their four-hour watch. It's a ritual nearly as old as the Navy itself.

Every workspace had its own coffee pot because the mess decks were off-limits during working hours and watchstanders aren't free to go off for a cup, anyway. But to actually wash the pot is un-heard of, frowned upon, not done, verboten, you get the idea.

So what did we do about the buildup of slimy brown residue on the inside of the urn, you ask? Well, about every six months, while making a fresh pot, some careless junior person would accidently lose the urn's lid over the side of the ship due to "high winds." The store-keepers didn't stock just the lids, only entire coffee pots, so we'd have to requisition a whole new pot. And because it had been six months since the last one was deep-sixed, no one remembered that the previous pot had been replaced for the same reason. The old, sludge-encrusted urn would then drift slowly down to Davy Jones' locker with the rest of the rubbish that all ships produce. (Remind me sometime to explain the difference between flotsam and jetsam, if you're interested.)

Once, during his weekly Friday afternoon inspection of work-ing and sleeping spaces, the ship's executive officer lifted the lid of our pot, frowned, and told me to see to it that it was washed immedi-ately and thoroughly. After he left, my boss, ST1 Andy Anderson, frowned, leaned back in his chair, looked off into space and reminded me that we'd had that pot for nearly six months, anyway. Andy was one of the people who hated the taste of soap in his coffee cup. Such a shame. I hated to report to him that the lid blew off and over the side while I was on my way to wash it.

CATHOLIC NIGHT

BY BOB COHEN

Food was an important part of the daily routine on the *USS Henry B. Wilson (DDG-7)*. That ship was nothing if not a good feeder. It seemed that even the worst of days could be brightened by hearing the happy cry of a shipmate discovering a routine day's dinner menu: "Yay! Sliders!"

While the food was great, the service superb and the price right, the same could not be said of the restaurant's ambiance — at least not when the captain was eating with us. He did do this from time to time; that is, to take a break from the eighteen-hour day he expected everyone to work right along with him, and sit down to a good meal.

The normally raucous wardroom was very quiet when the skipper was there. It's not that we didn't like him, it's just that... uh, everyone was a little afraid of him. Wardroom conversation with the captain was generally pleasant and trivial. We never talked shop, just philosophy. "Mr. Smith, what's the difference between *pulse width* and *pulse repetition rate*?" Or, "By the way, Mr. Jones, exactly what is the pressure inside the de-aerating feed tank?" The first time I saw him smile was about a year after I came aboard. Never before having seen his teeth bared, I thought he was going to bite me.

Dining with the captain was formal, to say the least. We adhered rigidly to all naval customs, traditions and etiquette. Had we eaten every day in choker whites it couldn't have been more stiff.

One of our standard dining practices was that on Friday nights there was no meat on the menu, only seafood. We informally referred to this as Catholic Night. Broiled fish, steamed clams, fried shrimp and lobster tails were all Friday night staples, and in the ways of the mariner, this gave us yet another way to mark our personal calendars and observe the passage of time — until the night the captain made his shocking announcement.

"Gentlemen, I've come to a decision," he said. The wardroom became even quieter than it was, if that was possible. Some of us actually stopped breathing in anticipation of whatever was coming. "This tradition of having only seafood on the menu every Friday is,

well, archaic. I think from now on, we'll just have a normal menu."
He sat back, and judging by the fact that he was smiling for at least
the second time on record, he was apparently quite pleased with himself. Despite this unusual display of benevolence there was no immediate response from the wardroom. As the silence became awkward,
there was a timid voice from the junior end of the table: "But Sir, we
like Catholic Night ..."

FEEDING THE CREW OF A TIN CAN

BY ARNOLD HOFMANN

"Hey Cookie, what's for lunch?" Feeding two hundred and
fifty enlisted men three to four meals a day on a *Gearing*-class destroyer with a half dozen cooks was big job. It was one of those jobs
where nothing was easy and as you finished one meal, preparation for
the next one would soon start. To make it a bit more challenging, the
designers of the *Gearing*-class put the galley on the main deck and
the serving line and mess decks one deck below so that all hot food
had to be muscled down a steep ladder.

In 1970, Commissaryman (CS) supply ratings cooked and
served food for the crew in the general mess, baked, ordered, invento-
ried and issued all food items aboard ship. They had a food budget
and they had to stick to it. In addition to the commissaryman, a petty
officer (first, second or third) from some other division in the ship
was assigned to work for the Supply Department for a period of
ninety days as Mess Deck Master at Arms. Also, there were about six
non-rated enlisted men from other departments who would work in
supply as Messcooks and report to the Mess Decks MAA. They
would assist in food preparation, operate the scullery and clean the
mess decks.

"Mess Gear," passed on the 1MC was the notice to all hands
that "Dinner for the Crew" wouldn't be far behind. Time to start sali-
vating and getting washed up for the noon meal. "Mess Gear" was
passed on the 1MC about fifteen minutes before "Dinner for the
Crew." When mess gear was sounded the relieving watchstanders and
the mess cooks and commissarymen would eat.

At the head of the chow line there was usually a MAA with a

number clicker taking a head count of eaters. Sometimes it was a mess cook or a commissaryman but there was always a head count taken. The reason for the count was twofold. First, was the ration allowance. In port, the ship was paid its ration allowance for the number of people who actually ate the meal. At sea, the ship was paid the ration allowance for the full compliment on board. This count dictated how much money the general mess was allowed to spend in any given quarter. For example, the ration allowance in 1970 was probably about $2.50 per person per day for each person who ate in port and for each person on board when underway (officers were not included in this allowance count). The Chief Commissaryman and the Supply Officer had to monitor the allowance versus dollars spent so that they wouldn't overspend the budget in any given quarter. Inventories were taken and returns submitted to Washington, DC every quarter.

Sometimes, if you could see that you were overspending, you would adjust the menu to less-expensive fare for the last week or two of the quarter in order to stay within budget. On the other hand, if you were flush with money toward the end of the quarter, you would see a proliferation of expensive menu items (steak and or lobster) so that you would spend it all.

The second reason for the head count was for the chief commissaryman to better estimate the number of portions to cook and thereby reduce waste and the possibility of overspending the food allowance.

The crew's menu was a 6-week cycle menu. The menu for the week ahead in the cycle would be slightly modified by the chief based on what fresh food was available, what specialty foods the ship may have gotten from an underway replenishment or in port, the weather, expected operations, or what he might have run out of, or even on having a BBQ on the helo deck. Each line item in the cycle menu was coded with a number that represented the Navy Card that was to be used in the preparation of that item. The modified menu would be approved by the supply officer and submitted to the executive officer for approval each week. All menu cards were based on 100 portions so the chief could assemble his cycle menu, review the cards for quantities of food required, check the requirements against his inventory and place an order for what was needed for a 90-day load out.

At the end of each meal, the Watch Captain, as the senior cook for that meal was called, would document the amount of leftovers for a particular menu item or estimate how much he was short of another menu item. This info was then used to plan for the amount of a particular menu item to cook the next time in order to reduce waste and still have enough prepared.

If liver and onions were on the menu, you would always have another option because out of a crew of 250, you might only have 50 takers for that item. The watch captain would also prepare extra food at the evening meal to be used for midrats to be served for the midnight-to-0400 watch and the guys coming off of the 2000-to-2400 watch. Only one cook and probably one messcook staffed the galley for midrats so some pre-preparation was necessary.

I've heard sailors tell stories about the old days when powdered eggs were the norm rather than the exception. We nearly always had fresh eggs on board. Powdered eggs were not a routine item. We had pretty good replenishment from the Mobile Logistic Support Force which would refuel us every few days and cycle out of Subic with FFV (fresh fruit and vegetables). Milk was always a problem because we could only carry enough for about 4-5 days from port. Sometimes the FFV was not in good condition when we would get it while out on the gun line supporting the troops on the beach so there would be periods of time without much variety. Apples and oranges were usually available. Ice cream would only be available for a few days because of limited freezer space.

Any given week might include pot roast, steaks, hamburger, pork chops, spaghetti, hot dogs, macaroni and cheese, fish and lamb with potatoes and rice and typically canned vegetables. There was always dessert. At sea we had a night baker who would bake sweet rolls and fresh bread and rolls every night. Lunch would have a hot meal choice and lunchmeat sandwich choices, grilled cheese and Reuben sandwiches. Soup was a regular item with meals. Breakfast was typically eggs to order, bacon, sausage, pancakes, chipped beef on toast, French toast, hot cereal, toast, canned juice, and fruit if available.

Feeding sailors was part of greasing the machinery that made the ship go.

"STARRY, STARRY NIGHT..."

BY ROBIN SMITH

Midwatches (0000 to 0400) might seem like a rough watch to stand, but I enjoyed them. After a long day of anti-submarine exercises, damage control drills, and other hectic evolutions, the midwatch was a relaxing time to be at sea. Surely, it was best to be in your rack snoring in harmony with sixty-six other sailors, but there are interesting things to see even in the midnight hours.

What can one see when it is pitch dark? Growing up in a rural area I thought I knew what dark was, but I would learn a new meaning of dark out in the middle of the ocean. There is no light on the bridge of a Navy ship with the exception of the galaxy of red glowing buttons and nebulous dials. These aren't much when it comes to illumination, but the most interesting lights are external to the bridge anyway.

The skies are so dark at sea that the colors of stars become apparent. Back home in Wisconsin the star Betelgeuse appeared no different than other stars that filled the light-polluted skies. At sea, however, the star shone orange, typical of a Red Giant star. Other stars displayed blues and greens, which are typical of very hot stars. Then there is the Milky Way. The Milky Way is an awesome sight once you can get away from the light pollution of inland and coastal areas. Various dark nebulae strewn along its length stand out like ominous storm clouds. A prime example is the Coal Sack Nebula. The Coal Sack looks like a hole punched through the Milky Way.

When you tired of watching the stars, the warm water of the tropics created its own constellation of stars. Bioluminescent creatures such as phytoplankton and diatoms glow in the wakes of the ship. Occasionally one of these critters glows exceptionally bright like a micro-super nova, and stands out from the other lesser lights. These little sparks of light are embedded in the foam of the wake that also glows with an eerie light. If the sonar is active, you can watch the sound waves disappear over the horizon in a heartbeat.

Topside decks can only be accessed at night through specially-designated watertight doors which are outfitted with baffles painted flat black. The bulkheads of the passageway opening out onto the deck are also painted flat black. These are often referred to as *light lockers.* From time to time when I wasn't on watch I would venture onto the 03 weather deck between the forward superstructure and the after superstructure to watch the heavens in their resplendent glory.

The first time I did this was quite an adventure. Walking through the red-lit passageway to the light locker I opened the door and stepped out onto the weather deck, dogging the door after me. I was immediately gripped by a bad case of vertigo. The dark gray of the deck was as black as the sky above. Although I could feel the deck beneath my feet, my mind rebelled at the lack of visual cues. The gentle rocking of the ship did not help me gather my bearings. I stood still, only an arm's length from the door I entered through, until my night vision came to me. As it did, I became aware of a faint glow casting a shadow of me on the deck at my feet. At first I thought this was created by the masthead light on the after mast. The masthead and range lights are only two of five lights to shine from a Navy ship at night, even in peacetime. These lights were positioned at the tops of the forward and after mast to allow other ships to determine our orientation relative to them at night. During war, even these lights would be extinguished. They were shielded, and only allowed viewing from specific angles. When I looked up to see what source of light was casting my shadow, these lights were not visible from where I stood. It was then I realized my shadow was being cast by starlight. Truly awesome. This feeble light served me well one dark evening when I was desperate for a celestial fix and had to seize any opportunity to shoot one. Starlight is sufficient to illuminate the horizon if night vision is properly preserved.

The stars were all but invisible during times of a full moon. Even so, the moon is a beautiful sight to see. The advantages of being at sea do not work to an observer's advantage since the moon shines quite brightly. There were times, however, when the moon hung over the horizon casting eerie reflections on the sea's surface. Throw in sounds from the ship's hydrophones and you have a scene right out of a "B" grade horror film.

Not all stars of the midwatch are natural in origin. Sailing up and down the coastal United States provides a scene filled with man-made lights for the sailor to watch and ponder. Sailing along the coast makes a midwatch a little more hectic since those beacons in the night allow for visual navigation and prominent land features are good for electronic navigation. There is still plenty of time to watch the lights of the city rise up off the forward quarter, and set a short time later on the stern quarter. These lights would make a homesick and lovesick sailor yearn to be ashore partying at the bars and dance halls whose marquees act like a siren's call. Those very same lights were a sailor's bane during WWII, when U-boat commanders used them to detect naval and merchant shipping transiting up and down the coast. The fires of sinking ships eventually led coastal cities to turn most, if not all, of their lights off for the duration.

Lovers walking the shores looking out to sea might notice some of the stars on the horizon, slowly marching across the night sky out of step with the other stars of the heavens. Those taking the time to interrupt their reverie to look seaward are often unaware of the sailors guarding their midnight stroll. Meanwhile, a lonely, weary sailor leans against the rail of the bridge wing longing to be among the bright lights of town.

The stars of the heavens and man continue to blaze when the midwatch comes to an end. Sailors dead on their feet return to their racks to catch a couple hours sleep before starting their day's work, only to be greeted by a different array of stars on their next midwatch.

WAKE ME WHEN THEY ORDER "SPLICE THE MAINBRACE"

BY DICK KING

I am not sure, but I think the phrase "Splice the Main Brace" is an archaic term for having a drink left over from the days of sail and the Royal Navy. But that is the order I got one night in the Gulf of Tonkin. How can that happen? What does it mean?

The first and primary commanding officer I served under was Commander (later Captain) G. G. Ely Kirk, a 1947 graduate of the Naval Academy. When I walked aboard he had been there two weeks and he was on his third command at sea, which included an LST, a DE and now a DD. On my second day when I first was interviewed by the captain, I asked for engineering duty, but he told me that wasn't possible. However, he promised me engineering duty as soon as a billet opened up and he kept his word. In the meantime, I went to Operations and learned a lot. In retrospect I believe that every junior officer should serve in two different departments in their first three years.

Sometime late in 1967 I became first an OOD/I (Officer of the Deck Independent) and then an OOD/F (Fleet). The first classification allowed me to drive the ship at sea when we were by ourselves. The OODF classification meant that I was allegedly qualified to drive the *Chevalier* while in various formations, including the most dangerous, the "3C2" used with three destroyers and an aircraft carrier. Most destroyer captains were very uptight about qualifying people, but Kirk was kind of laid back. I became a fairly good OODF in the Gulf of Tonkin, but that is not to mean that I was really ready for all the danger there. Shortly after becoming an OODF and while standing a morning watch (0400 – 0800) with a bunch of ships, the senior officer present afloat and his staff cranked out the most convoluted op-order I have ever seen. It had twenty warships converging on three unrep ships in the dark to take on, respectively, fuel, ammunition and supplies.

Before sunrise, the officer who designed this crazy and dangerous maneuver gave the order by voice radio paraphrased as best I can remember, "Abandon your assigned station and take station on your first unrep ship." Wow! It was dark out there and I couldn't tell one unrep ship from another. Every night in the Night Orders, it said wake the captain whenever the situation looked confusing or dangerous or involved passing another ship at less than 2,000 yards, but I had learned from the school of hard knocks that if I woke the captain on those criteria, he would be pissed. It was a CYA thing put in writing with a different message transmitted subtly. What was written in the night orders was not what he really wanted.

I must admit I didn't have a clue which unrep ship was which. I reached the point where I thought we (meaning me as Officer of the Deck and my CIC watch which was trying hard to sort the situation out) were totally confused. I decided it was time to wake the captain. So I entered Captain Kirk's sea cabin and woke him up. After a minute or so he came out to the bridge in his bathrobe and Weejuns and sat in his chair. He asked for a cup of coffee, which was quickly provided from CIC. Then he started looking at all of the lights from ships that were visible. He started asking, "what ship is that," and he would point.

I had to answer in most cases, "I don't know, sir."

Then he started listening to the radio, specifically the Pri-Tac circuit (UHF) that was used between ships in formation. The situation was so screwed up that after ten minutes, he didn't have a better picture of what was going on than I did. Then he did a strange thing and possibly a dangerous thing. He stood up and told me he was going back to bed and I was to wake him when they ordered, "Splice the Main Brace."

My Captain, my Captain, where art thou when I need you? But ship-by-ship, CIC and the signalmen identified the key ships, including the first of the three unrep ships we were to go alongside that morning (one each for fuel, stores and ammo). It was still dark and frankly I was scared and a nervous wreck. It was a cool morning but I was really sweating. Somehow without colliding with any other ship, I managed to maneuver the *Chevalier* 100 yards astern and slightly to starboard of the first of our unrep ships. At first light, the unrep ship hoisted a signal indicating *prepare to come alongside*. By now the XO was on the bridge getting in the way (he was useless) but as he jabbered at me I called away the Special Sea and Unrep Detail and went again to wake the captain. In his sea cabin I told him, "We are ready to go alongside sir, and *Romeo* was half-blocked." He said he would be right out.

Normal procedure at that point would have been for the more experienced Special Sea and Unrep Detail OOD to relieve me; I was mentally exhausted and physically tired and was really looking forward to speaking those magic words "I stand relieved."

Captain Kirk reappeared on the bridge, now dressed in khakis but still wearing his regulation Bass Weejuns, and then blew my mind for the second time that morning. "Mr. King, you got us here, you may as well take us alongside."

Oh, shit! First of all, I had never done that before. Visions of disaster and catastrophe danced through my head. But I had watched the exercise many times before and essentially knew what to do.

The signal flag was suddenly *two blocked* and I ordered 25 knots — Kirk liked to go alongside smartly. As we approached the alongside position I crashed back on the speed and soon the lines started going over. I am standing on the port wing of the bridge giving a bunch of orders trying to keep the ship in place and avoiding the catastrophe that I was certain was going to happen. Things settled out a bit, and although it was probably not the smoothest unrep ship approach the *Chevalier* had done, so far no disaster. Kirk was coaching a bit, but very little. He would get too distracted over other things like talking to the CO of the unrep ship, choosing which movies we wanted to exchange, and other important issues like that. I was now really mentally and physically exhausted and wished this torture would end. After what seemed liked hours, but which was probably about one hour, we were finished and I rang up 27 knots to break away (with the ship's band playing loudly) in Captain Kirk's signature style.

At that point I headed for the second unrep ship. I recall that I reminded the captain at that point that I had been on continuous OOD watch since 0345 and it was now after 0900. He got the point and I was finally relieved. I watched the rest of that unrep from the safety of the after engineroom. I loved that after engineroom!

Footnote: On *Sumners* and *Gearings* in the sixties we did not have enough quartermasters on board for the luxury of using them as helmsmen. It took every quartermaster we had to work the navigation problem. So the routine steaming helmsmen were usually in 1st Division and from that pool came the special sea detail helmsmen based on officer recommendations as to who were best. For a while, perhaps even in the above-described unrep, we had a YNSN (the log room yeoman no less) as a qualified special sea detail helmsman.

I'M IN A GEARING FRAM OF MIND OR RANDOM RECOLLECTIONS OF LIFE ON A TIN CAN

BY DAVE CARLSON

In 1977 I was stationed aboard *USS Spruance (DD-963)*. She was brand-new then, the first of her kind. She was clean, fast, and THE class of can to be on. But after our new CO ripped fifty feet of rubber off the sonar dome while trying to dock the ship, I decided to move.

I had requested no-cost orders so I could go the West Coast. When my orders came, they were for the *USS McKean (DD-784)*. A lot of sailors would have considered this to be purgatory. The *McKean* was a *Gearing*-class destroyer. A World War Two leftover, she was already past her 32nd birthday. She would be without any of *Spruance's* luxury items. I couldn't have cared less.

The *McKean* was a veteran of three wars, she had more salt on her bridge than the *Spruance* had in total, and she was living, breathing history. I reported aboard in November of 1977. She was in the Lockheed Shipyard at the time, so she didn't have her make-up on when I saw her for the first time. It didn't matter. She had a look about her that said, "Hi, how ya doin'?" She was a ship who was comfortable with her past and didn't need to prove anything to anyone.

The *McKean* was a FRAM can. Which is to say, she had been re-built in the sixties under the Fleet Rehabilitation And Modernization program so that she would remain a useful fighting ship and offer her crew a little more comfort. Her original clean sleek lines had been replaced with an enlarged superstructure, but she was still a beautiful ship.

Let's talk about life on a FRAM. It was *not* regular Navy. By the time I served on the *McKean*, she had become part of the Naval Reserve Force. We were an active naval unit, but we were manned at about 60% of full-crew level. That meant more work for everyone. The *McKean* was an old girl. She had cramped living quarters with canvas racks, equipment that needed constant love and attention, and a constant hunt for spare parts to keep the old girl going. But, it also meant a very tight crew who liked each other, worked and played well together, and who interacted from department to department far more cheerfully than most ships. We knew we were all in the same situation — short on staff, short on parts. It brings a crew together when they have to face a little daily adversity. It also made our daily triumphs sweeter. I firmly believe we had one of the greatest collections of jokers, scam artists, bullshitters, and pirates ever assembled on one naval vessel. Parts not obtainable through "normal channels" were found elsewhere.

Meals aboard the *McKean* were also an adventure. Because we were a reserve can, we were at pretty much the bottom of the navy supply chain. As a rule, we ran out of fresh eggs, milk, fruit, veggies and juice within forty-eight hours of "Underway, shift colors." We often dined on that wonderful gastronomical treat known as "McKean Mystery Meat." Sometimes, we had a little ham with the fat. The snipes often stopped by the galley to collect the spare grease that floated on the SOS for use as lube oil. No big deal, it just gave us cast-iron stomachs. We often had a floor show with our meals. This was the chief corpsman making his way through the messdecks with his sprayer, making another futile attempt at cockroach suppression.

Sometimes our operations were simple drudge work, like plane-guard duty. But sometimes we got to be inventive. During one squadron exercise, we were elected to be the "Bad Guy." Our job was to avoid running afoul of the rest of Desron 37 and to inflict as much damage on them as we could. During one night operation, someone came up with the notion of camouflaging the ship. To do this, we strung every work light we had topside, opened up as many doors as we could with the darken ship screens retracted, and then turned on all the white lights inside and out. We turned off all the radars except for the navigational radar. We were encouraged to wander the decks in and out of uniform. The purpose of all this was to make ourselves look like a commercial vessel, and it worked, we steamed right through the squadron and they never knew who we were until it was too late.

Gearings could haul ass when they were allowed to. Once during transit to San Diego we had to take off after a downed F-14 pilot. The snipes got word to superheat and we went to 34 knots *right now.* It's always a treat to watch your ship throwing a rooster tail.

FRAMs handled well, and she rode well. In heavy seas, the weather decks, especially the main deck, were to be avoided. We routinely had green water breaking against Mount 51. Rollers would run down the main deck from stem to stern. Get grabbed by one and you'd better have a good grip on a handrail or lifeline or you might just become history. If you think tin can sailors are joking when they bitch about wanting sub pay, think again.

We got to go to liberty ports the bigger ships couldn't even dream of. We once went into Humboldt Bay for a port call in Eureka, California. What a liberty port that was! The high school band was waiting for us at the pier playing "Anchors Aweigh" and the "Star Wars" theme. For three days, our money was worthless as the town opened up to us. Try doing *that* with a cruiser.

Because we were a tight crew, there was a lot more mingling of officers and enlisted while on liberty. I very clearly remember a time in Victoria, British Columbia, when, while seeing the city, I climbed onto a city bus to be greeted by, "Hey! There's Carlson! Yay!" At the back of the bus were two thirds of the junior officers, absolutely bagged. They had just come from some bar where they had exacted revenge on the crew of a Canadian destroyer. It seems the night before, the Canucks had invited them over to their ship for "a few pints" and had promptly drank our officers under the table using Guiness as the weapon of choice. Our wardroom responded the next day, after recovering, by inviting the Canadians out for cocktails. The report I received was that they had left the Canucks passed out in a bar.

We had almost no political climbers on the *McKean.* There was too much work to do to play those games. Anyone who was a climber was instantly marked by the crew and shunned as far as shipboard life would allow. The only exception that I know of was our CO in '79. He had somehow gotten in the dog house and was hoping to get out by volunteering us for any assignment he could.

So what was life like on a FRAM? It was hard work, long hours, and crappy living conditions. It was great and you made lifelong friends. It was watching rollers come at you from astern whose tops were five feet over your head. It was liberty call until 0300 hours and, "Turn to, commence ships work," just four hours later. In short, it was the very definition of being a Tin Can Sailor: "Work hard, play harder."

... AND A STAR TO STEER HER BY

BY ROBIN SMITH

"All I ask is tall ship, and a star to steer her by!" — *John Masefield*

In 1974 as my high school graduation approached and I began contemplating my future, a recruiter and I discussed a possible naval career. I had been fascinated by the Brown Water Navy (riverine patrol craft) but by then the war in 'Nam was all but over, and they had packed up and moved home. I wanted to fly, but schooling (or lack thereof), and nearsightedness squashed that dream. The only other way to find fulfillment was to do the East Coast with the hopes of getting to see Northern Europe at some point in my career.

I became a part of the *USS Spruance (DD-963)* commissioning crew after Quartermaster "A" school in August. Built in Pascagoula, Mississippi, and commissioned there in September of '75, we set about putting her through her paces. A good, thorough shakedown kept us busy for the better part of a year. A trip to Europe seemed far off, and it seemed more likely a trip to the Med would happen first. Fortunately, King Neptune smiled upon me and in the fall of '77 we prepared to sail for Northern Europe for some NATO ops.

The *Spruance* belonged to the *USS America (CV-66)* Battle Group, which left without us. We had managed to mangle one of our prop shafts during one of our port of calls in the Caribbean, and we had to make a detour to the Philadelphia NSY to get it replaced. The Special Sea and Anchor detail into Philly was a very long but straightforward one. This transit was done in daylight, and would be nothing like what I would experience in the weeks to come. In no time, the shaft was replaced, and we were kicked out the gate, and on our way. I laid out my great circle route, and the captain made up for lost time as we headed alone across the pond.

About mid-way a Russian Tu-64 "Bear" intercepted us. The "Snoopy Team" (intelligence gathering team) was called away to take some family photos for the scrap album as we continued on our way. We caught up to the Battle Group in Lisbon, Portugal. The crew was allowed a night of liberty there before setting sail again the next morning. There was no time to get into trouble.

The North Atlantic gave us a good show with high winds and impossible seas. I learned a valuable lesson in navigating through a storm when we were to stay on station doing a racetrack route. Unfortunately, the Officer of the Deck (OOD) and I neglected to take into account the *Spruance's* huge sail area and allowed ourselves to be blown a good distance away from our station by the time we received orders to move on. The CO was none too pleased, and we finished our watch with our tails between our legs.

The next day the skies cleared and the seas calmed down. We found ourselves with our group, and formed up with our NATO allies. During one phase of the exercise, we took an "enemy" surface force under fire. The *Spruance* radioed, "guns-guns-guns," to announce a salvo, but the *HMS Kent (D-12)* decided a touch of reality was needed. Using no bullets, she loaded her guns with powders, and let them rip. I notified the OOD (a naval academy grad) that the *Kent* was firing off our rear port quarter. The OOD was standing at the centerline pelorus, and gave me a wide-eyed stare as if he thought I had lost all my senses. He made it to the bridge wing in about three steps, and was promptly greeted with a large "boom!" from the *Kent's* forward turret. Much to my surprise, he made his way back to his station as quickly as he left it, and carried on as if nothing of interest happened. On, with the games!

The operations were concluded the next day with the Blue Force declared the winner (you have to love scripted warfare), and we bid our British mates, "Cheerio!" The next stop was the Baltic, with a side trip to Oslo, Norway, so we made our way through the Channel and into the North Sea.

The North Sea failed to live up to its reputation and proved to be the smoothest part of the cruise. The winds were light and the seas as calm as they are in the doldrums. We moved into the Skagerrak, north of Jutland, and headed to Oslo, Norway. This was my dream come true. I was going to visit the homeland of my maternal grandfather. We had our pre-sea and anchor detail briefing to discuss the up and coming navigational problem. Nobody had been to Oslo before, so no one knew what to expect. What made this worse is that the time of our transit up the fjord would be early morning, and during December the sun wouldn't rise until after ten. So, we were going to be in a tight spot with no light to show us the way, not even stars since they would be directly overhead, the horizon obscured by the walls of the fjord. The same steep walls would also hide all navigation aids, which would pop up and disappear without warning.

The chart and radar showed the approach to the mouth of the fjord. As we expected, it was pitch black and the walls of the fjord were invisible to the naked eye, save for an occasional light from a house on the mountainside. Radar wasn't going to be much help this time, since the steep walls produce too much clutter. Anything useful for navigation would be visible to our radar and bearing takers simultaneously, so radar wasn't going to give us any edge. Our Quartermaster gang consisted of two QM2s, including myself, and three seamen (one non-rated). With one on the helm, one on the logbook, an assistant navigator and a phone talker, we were short a bearing taker or two. Fortunately, we had trained some Radioman-types to supplement the force and we were good to go. The RMs actually enjoyed shooting bearings, since they got to watch us come into port.

We made our way slowly up the fjord, our eyes alert for beacons and other nav-aids. Snow on the slopes was visible with what little light shone from houses and such, but there was little else to see. Radar told us enough to "stay between the lines," but not much more. The chart made it look like we had some wiggle room, but you felt awfully claustrophobic with the side of the fjord lurking there in the dark.

While we were encountering no difficulties, the pucker factor was up at least two notches. The main sweat pumps were on 1-slow/1-fast. Suddenly, the Navigator announced that he was striking below to change into his blues. He told the other 2nd class petty officer to do the same, and left me in charge of the nav-team. I was up to the challenge, but the pucker factor just got higher, and the main sweat pumps were now on 2-fast.

Things were going smoothly. The bearing takers were hitting their marks. The markers, buoys and beacons came into view about when we expected them to. Sct and drift were being calculated and forwarded up to the OOD who was skillfully keeping us in mid-channel. Still, I was ever on my toes waiting for the unexpected.

Then, according to Admiral Murphy's Law, the unexpected happened! The navigator returned to the bridge and stepped up to my right side. Up to this point everything had run smoothly. As I turned toward the navigator to give him the update, I look past him to see lights moving rapidly from aft to fore. For a split second it looked as if the helmsman had gone nuts and put on hard right rudder, and was heading us into the walls of the fjord. Blood rushed from my head, and my knees began to buckle. Before losing consciousness, I realized that what I was seeing was an optical illusion; it was just a merchant ship passing us on the starboard side. I had been either too intent on my job to have heard any information about this ship passing us, or no one had bothered to tell me. With an audible sigh of relief, I regained my composure and continued with my report. I struck below to change uniforms (and underwear) then returned to the bridge, manning the starboard pelorus.

By the time we hit the Oslo harbor, filled with ice floes, we were in the middle of Civil Twilight. It was 0900 and sunrise was still over an hour away. Oslo was a beautiful city, cloaked in a powdery layer of snow. We took in the sights, which included a medieval castle. This castle served as a prison during WWII and was home to Quisling, the Norwegian traitor. The night before departing for the Baltic, the American Embassy threw the crew a party, and invited some young ladies to make our evening more enjoyable. We were all anxious to meet some sweet Scandinavian women and wasted little time in making their acquaintance. A buddy and I fortified ourselves then sallied forth. Speaking slowly, and clearly, we introduced ourselves, and asked a pair of ladies to dance. To our surprise they spoke perfect English. It turned out they were exchange students from Minnesota. Nuts! But, they were cute, blond and eager to dance, so we swallowed our disappointment and enjoyed their company.

We left Oslo under the morning sun, and the sight of the fjord was breathtaking. It was much more comfortable the second time around with daylight to help us find our way! I'll go back some day, but next time I'll fly.

HAVE YOU HUGGED A PETTY OFFICER LATELY?

BY MIKE SNYDER

We were at sea aboard a destroyer in the Mediterranean in the front third of a six- to nine-month deployment. There was a tentative knock on my stateroom door. From my desk I hollered, "come in," and turned to greet whoever entered. Into the room stepped a first class Fire Control Technician I knew as a good petty officer, a fine technician, and a solid individual. He was the key to the operation and maintenance of our main battery, the ship's missile fire control system, and he bore his responsibilities well. Immediately I recognized a stress I had never seen in him before. He asked, "Do you have a few minutes? I need to talk to you." He was obviously under a tremendous tension.

I waved him in to the only other chair in the room, reached over and pushed the door closed. After a slight pause he said, "I need to go home." His voice was shaky and he had trouble looking me in the eye. He was very agitated. He wrung his hands and formed smooth little creases in his dungaree trousers.

I had heard similar words from others, but they were a real surprise coming from this man. I responded by asking if there was something wrong at home; an emergency or death the command didn't know about. He married about a year before and his wife had recently given birth to their first child. The ship had been in its work-up cycle over the previous six months with lots of underway periods for training prior to deployment. Though he was home when the baby was born, we left for the Med very soon afterward. "I can't stand being away from my family. They need me. I don't know how they're getting along without me," he said. I questioned him about problems at home. There were none. He hadn't received a Dear John and he had complete confidence in his wife's trust, strength, and abilities.

I empathized with this man. I had had similar feelings shortly after I was married. I recall being overwhelmed by the requirements of sea duty and the enormity of providing a sound and secure home for my wife and our child, all on the very limited income of an E-5. At the time I felt I was alone and had to do it all. My confidence in my ability to provide for them was shaky, and I wasn't there to ensure they were well on a day-to-day basis.

Not long into our conversation he completely broke down. Sobbing into his hands, his shoulders shook uncontrollably. He stood and tried to look away, but there was no place to go. Instinctively, I stood as he did. The free space in the room was only four feet by six feet, and now it held two men and two chairs. We were very close. Without conscious thought, the naval officer persona melted away, compassion replacing whatever reserve I might have had. I took him in my arms and without speaking, held him the few moments it took for his weeping to subside. With tears streaming down his face he apologized while attempting to regain his composure. I patted him on the back a few times, gave his shoulder a squeeze, and guided him back into the chair. We all have our limits. He had simply reached his this day.

We talked for a long time after that. I shared my experiences with him and discussed the support that existed at home in the ships wives organization and the more formal things through the chaplain's offices. We worked through the facts that his wife had not expressed any concern in recent mail; that all communications indicated things with her and the baby were going well, and he had put their financial affairs in order before getting underway. I encouraged him to share his thoughts and emotions in letters to her. I also told him I would get him ashore to make a phone call immediately upon mooring in our next port call. As the conversation waned I urged him to wash his face and hands in the little sink in my room. We shook hands. He said thanks and left in better spirits, I think. Neither of us mentioned that meeting again.

A week later he "escorted" the supply officer and postal clerk ashore in the first boat and made a phone call home. Still later, in a private moment on deck, he told me his family was okay. In the following months he took and passed the fleet exam for Chief. He was selected and promoted before I left the ship. I think he stayed in the Navy for a full tour. But that had nothing to do with my motivation for acting as I had. He was a shipmate in trouble who needed someone to listen. I'm pleased I was there to help.

QUOTH THE LIEUTENANT, EVERMORE

BY TERRY MILLER

Like servicemen everywhere, I suppose, those aboard a gunship in a combat zone come up with unexpected ways of dealing with the odd combination of stress of potential fights and boredom of waiting between them. One, at least, was one of my ship's officers, a lieutenant aboard the destroyer, *George K. MacKenzie (DD-836)*.

For those who weren't in the Navy, let me explain that nearly everyone "stands watch" in addition to his regular duties. He mans a particular position for a four hour period each day and sometimes more than once a day. A sonar technician, I "stood" my watch by sitting in a tiny darkened room operating the sonar equipment in rotation with another sonarman in 20 minute segments to avoid fatigue and the possibility of missing an unfriendly submarine. Most officers, other than the commanding officer, his executive officer, and the supply officer, quite literally stood their four-hour shift on the bridge (the command and control area), also in pairs, as Officer of the Deck and Junior Officer of the Deck in charge of the entire ship and its activities.

During the eight-to-midnight segment of these periods of unequal parts of tedium and tension, especially when boredom had become so unbearable that stress began to look good, was when the lieutenant would entertain the other eight men on the bridge by reciting long poems from memory. Among the poems he chose to recite was Edgar Allan Poe's "The Raven." He'd walk around the bridge area, never stumbling over a word, orating as if he were on stage. So entertaining were his renditions that Combat Information Center and Sonar, coupled to the bridge by a special telephone circuit, would be told so that the off-duty watchstanders could go to the bridge and catch the lieutenant's act.

In another diversion a different officer, my own division's boss in fact, chose to work with bad weather and rough seas to further the stomach distress of the approximately one-third of the bridge watchstanders who suffered from seasickness. He would take out one of the big green cigars he smoked only on such occasions, light it with great fanfare, and walk around the bridge, puffing a trail of that greasy kind of cigar smoke that permanently clings even to metal and stains paper and clothing. After the stench had had time to bring many in his audience to a shade of green equal to his cigar, he would announce in a loud voice, "Man, I could go for a big glass of raw egg and warm mayonnaise!" This declaration was usually followed by one or two swollen-cheeked men, fingers pressed to their lips, diving for the doors to the outside so that they could "man the rails." While it may seem cruel in retrospect, it did serve to alleviate the stress and the boredom, and even the fear that inevitably accompanies those in a ship in stormy seas. Those he affected might still disagree.

But one of my fellow sonarmen decided during a storm that he would plagiarize our lieutenant with his own cigar. Puffing away on the foul smelling stogie as he stood in a group of younger sailors, he only got out, "Man, I could go for a ... Big ... gla ..." before making his own mad dash for the side of the ship. Word of this event was also passed around on the telephone circuit for days and days.

THE FIX

BY ROBIN SMITH

Today you can purchase a reasonably priced Global Positioning System (GPS) receiver and always know where you are. You can even buy a car with a navigation system that can literally tell you how to "get there from here!" GPS operates a constellation of 24 satellites, and it's rare that fewer than five are in your field of view at any one time, meaning position updates are real time. GPS receivers cannot only tell you where you are, but which direction you're moving, the distance covered and your speed. It would seem that navigators and Navy quartermasters are a thing of the past. Certainly, their jobs have become greatly simplified.

During my time aboard the *Spruance*, from 1975 to 1978, the navigation team had the use of a number of devices to determine our position. Visual bearings on landmarks along the shore provided position information through triangulation. Range data was also available using radar, which was also useful for triangulating objects beyond visual range. Celestial Navigation was used, weather permitting. Sun lines and stars allowed us to locate our position whenever the sky was clear enough. For all other occasions the *Spruance* was equipped with the predecessor to GPS, NAVSTAR, and the successor to LO-RAN-C, which was called OMEGA. NAVSTAR was the navy's constellation of six navigation satellites, and it wasn't uncommon to go several hours without a good fix. As for OMEGA, well, suffice it to say that LORAN-C is still in use. Our OMEGA system was, in principle, identical to LORAN-C (radio navigation), but was to have wider coverage with fewer transmitter stations. The only time our OMEGA system worked was when our second CO asked why we never used it. Naturally, he wanted a demonstration, and, according to Murphy's Law, it worked perfectly, but just that one time!

It wasn't necessary to obtain a visual, celestial or electronic fix on our position on a continuous basis. Dead Reckoning (DR) worked sufficiently well to determine position, with only occasional updates. This was particularly true during independent steaming (going from point A to point B) and calm winds. However, heavy weather and/or vigorous maneuvering meant that dead reckoning would rapidly lose accuracy, and more frequent fixes became necessary. This wasn't normally a problem, but there is always the exception!

During a training sortie in the Virginia Capes Operations Area (VACAPES OPAREA), we were busily conducting engineering drills, battle station drills, damage control drills, etc., all the while turning circles in the ocean. All went well until the end of the training cycle and it was time to start considering heading for the barn. During the final days a front moved in and celestial navigation was impossible due to the overcast. We were better than a hundred miles from shore, which ruled out radar or visual navigation. OMEGA was never considered, and the satellites were not in a favorable position to obtain a good fix. After more than a day without a solid fix, we were concerned that our dead reckoning was not accurate by any stretch of the imagination. When you're expected at the sea buoy at a specific time, and along the pier shortly thereafter, you better know which way to steer and how fast to paddle! About all we could say at this point was, "We are off the east coast!" Not a statement that builds confidence in your abilities among the crew. Nor does it win you friends when everyone is anxious to return to the bosom of their loving families.

As evening approached the day before we were to return, the clouds were solid overcast. A celestial fix wasn't "in the stars!" In an act of desperation, I suggested to the Navigator, as his senior quartermaster and assistant, that if the sky should open up in the middle of the night that we could get a star fix then. That notion didn't seem worth the effort in the navigator's estimation, and he declined. However, there was nothing forbidding me from doing it. Before hitting the rack, I left word with the Quartermaster of the Watch that should the skies clear, I was to be called. Shortly after midnight, the call came.

The messenger of the watch was shaking my shoulders, and whispering, "Smitty, they want you on the bridge!" All I could see was the glare from his flashlight, which, fortunately, was fitted with a red lens. I said, "Okay! I'll be right there!" I had taken with me a set of night-vision goggles. These were goggles with red lenses designed to help preserve night vision. Those were the first to go on, then my uniform. Normally, after sundown the ships internal lights are switched to red. This helped preserve the night vision of the watch standers, but there were always sources of white light, such as the galley, that were to be avoided, especially in this instance. For this to succeed, my night vision had to be perfect.

I arrived on the bridge, and sidled up alongside my striker to assess our reckoned position, and the clarity of the stars and horizon. The sky was clear and, amazingly, the horizon was visible, albeit barely. I took our predicted position and went to the chart house to select my stars and compute their predicted elevations and azimuths. Next, I tuned in the radio station WWV, which broadcasts the Universal Time (Coordinated) and set a stopwatch. Satisfied that the watch was set, I turned out all the red lights, and sat in the dark chart house for 30 minutes. This was necessary to ensure that my night vision was as good as it could be. The only light was the feeble glow from my watch. After time was up I grabbed my equipment and returned to the bridge.

Normally, star shots are taken during nautical twilight, which starts about thirty minutes after sunset. This provided sufficient light to see the horizon and record the sighting information, while allowing a clear view of the selected stars. We also normally had two "shooters," the navigator and me, as well as the recorder. This time I was shooting by myself, which was better considering how this was going to be done. Since it was dark, and I needed to preserve my night vision, I would hand my striker the sextant, who would then read it with his flashlight while I looked away. Had there been two of us, the time necessary to complete the sightings would have been much longer. As it was the going was slow, since now many more stars were visible than normal, and the horizon was not strikingly clear. Still, I made my sightings in short order, and returned to the chart house to reduce the data.

After I plotted the resulting fix on the chart, it revealed what we had feared. It did not agree at all well with our DR position. I notified the Officer of the Deck, who came to inspect my results. Unfortunately, the OOD had more confidence in our dead reckoning than my celestial fix. I respectfully pointed out that after a lengthy period of anti-submarine operations involving frequent changes in course and speed that the accuracy of our DR plot was in serious question. In spite of my insistence that my star shots were good, he did not relent, and ordered that we not use my celestial fix as a valid update to our position. I replied, "Aye, Sir!" then turned to the ship's deck log. I entered the coordinates of my celestial fix, followed by the written comment, "Rejected by OOD."

I did not do this out of spite. Although I was confident in my fix, it was the OOD's prerogative to accept or reject the fix and I didn't take the decision personally. At the same time, this was a legal issue, and an entry was required regardless of the decision.

The clouds had returned before the sun rose, and the situation was none the better. We would shortly have to turn for home, and we didn't have a warm and fuzzy feeling for which way that would be. This time, the navigator had a brainstorm, and came up with a method that was as unorthodox as my midnight star fix. He pulled out our high precision bathymetry charts and laid them out on the chart house table. We then returned to the bridge and noted the times we crossed specified fathom curves as indicated on our fathometer over the bridge chart table. Satisfied we had enough information we returned to the chart house and the bathymetry charts. Along the edge of a separate piece of paper, the navigator made marks at intervals based upon the chart scale, the recorded times and our speed. Then, the navigator tried to line the marks up with the proper curves on the chart. It looked like he was working a Ouija board as he slid that piece of paper around. Finally, the marks lined up with the curves and our position was recorded and plotted on the navigation chart on the bridge. As I discovered a few hours earlier, we were way off the mark!

One last step remained. Since the method of obtaining this fix was a bit unusual, its accuracy needed to be verified. So, we worked the DR track backwards from our new position to my star fix. This was done more as a double-check than a need for personal satisfaction. Nonetheless, I was greatly satisfied when the DR plot ran right across my star fix. The navigator made the recommended course and speed changes, and we sailed homeward.

Even though we had been gone a relatively short time, less than two weeks, families anxiously awaited our return. As the tugs came along side to nestle us into our berth and the D & S piers, wives, children and girlfriends waved to their sailors from the pier. Finally, the 1MC announced, "Moored! Shift Colors!" At that instant the flag at the main stay was hauled down, and another flag was raised from the flagstaff on the fantail, and the ensign at the jackstaff. The gangplank came across the quarterdeck and sailors headed home with their families, none of whom were aware that this homecoming was very close to being late!

Reflections

SPRUANCE CLASS

Length: 563' Displacement: 7800 tons 31 built, in service 1975-2005

QM2 Robin Smith
NX Division, USS Spruance (DD-963) 1974-78*

FTG2 Dave Carlson
Fox Division, USS Spruance (DD-963) 1974-77*

* pre-commissioning – Plankowners

THE COURT MARTIAL OF LIEUTENANT (J.G.) RICHARD H. KING, USNR

BY DICK KING

By April 1968, I was less than sixty days from completing my three-year obligation to the United States Navy. I had chosen not to augment (go "career") because I had been accepted to law school in the fall. One day the XO handed me a set of orders that directed me to report to Treasure Island in San Francisco for separation by a date certain, sometime in May or early June. The *USS Chevalier (DD-805)* was in the middle of an overhaul at Mare Island Naval Shipyard. I stuck the orders in my desk drawer.

During an overhaul, the MPA (Main Propulsion Assistant – my job) is one of the busiest junior officers on a ship, because M and B Division collectively have the most work orders. To add insult to injury, the new captain made me the "Tool Officer" for the entire ship, even after I suggested strongly that other junior officers on board had almost nothing to do during an overhaul, such as the CIC Officer or some of the weapons types. To further compound my workload, the new chief engineer was having all sorts of personal problems ashore and took thirty days leave followed later by thirty more days emergency leave. So I became the acting chief engineer for most of that summer.

But there were some good things going on in addition to my workload. The *Chevalier* had been declared uninhabitable, so I was receiving a small housing allowance which when combined with the allowance of two other junior officers, was more than enough to rent a nice two-bedroom garden apartment with a pool. We were in five duty sections. The San Francisco Bay area is a great place for a young bachelor and I was very content, almost as content as the prior summer on South Mission Beach in San Diego.

Law school didn't start until after Labor Day, and from time to time, I would look at my orders and ponder the question, what am I going to do this summer while waiting for law school to start if I return to Nashville? Check out groceries for the local grocery chain? Drive a forklift for the paper company? I was a bit old to do that again. At some point I decided, screw the orders. I was going to plug along as usual until thrown off the ship bodily and/or the paychecks stopped coming.

On the first payday after the "drop-dead date" for reporting to Treasure Island for separation, I waited nervously in the wardroom after breakfast. The Supply Officer came in to distribute the paychecks. "Dick, here is your check." This went on for weeks and weeks and no one said a word. I continued to stand CDO watches, carry out my duties as the Acting Chief Engineer, run herd over the ongoing engineering overhaul and inventory daily all of the shipyard-owned tools checked out to the *Chevalier*.

In the bilges of the engineering spaces, there is a maze of piping, including fuel oil piping that connects all of the twenty-some-odd fuel tanks via manifolds to the six oil pumps and then to the boiler fronts. Many of the sections of pipe were connected with flanges, and to repair them, ship's force could remove them, carry them to a tender or SRF shop, pick up the new ones a few days later and re-install. But whenever a pipe passed through a watertight bulkhead, the pipe was integrally welded to the bulkhead. These short sections were called "stub pipes" and their repair was a shipyard job.

Twice during the last WestPac cruise, we experienced a fuel oil stub pipe failure, in one case behind a steaming boiler. High pressure NSFO (Navy Special Fuel Oil) spewed everywhere, including on exposed steam pipe flanges that were 850-degrees Fahrenheit. Trust me, it was a scary moment in the fireroom. To repair the piping while underway, we would take *marlin*, a common shipboard waxed twine used for many purposes, and wrap the pipe at the leak point around and around and around and around, sort of like fixing a bad leak with duct tape.

Prior to leaving San Diego for the overhaul, I had prepared a shipyard work request asking for (a) x-ray or ultra-sound test all fuel oil stub piping, and (b) replacement as necessary. At the Pre-Arrival Conference, three tables were arranged in a triangle at COMCRUDESPAC (Commander, Cruisers Destroyers Pacific). The ship's representatives sat at one table, the Type Commander's representatives sat at another and the shipyard representatives sat at the third. I was one of the ship's representatives.

I presented and explained the fuel oil stub piping request to the conference, the shipyard reps kerplunked and kerplunked on their old analog calculators and somehow came up with an estimated cost. The Admiral, COMCRUDESPAC, then agreed to pay for it, and by implication at least, the shipyard agreed to do it. It was stamped "approved" in my sight and presence.

Mid-way through the overhaul, I realized that the shipyard hadn't even started on that job. I made frequent and polite inquiries to the appropriate shop and was told that it would be started soon. But more weeks passed and it was not started. BTC Richard Morton and I brought the subject up with the new chief engineer, during one of those few times he was on board. Someone recalled that in "BSTM" (Bureau of Ships Technical Manual, a multi-volume manual that served as the engineer's bible), three types of testing were allowed on fuel oil piping. There was the x-ray test, the ultrasound test and then there was the old fashioned "hammer test." Using a standard chipping hammer, tap on the pipe at suspected weak points, and if the hammer penetrated the pipe, it had to be replaced (how about that for logic). The new chief engineer supposedly talked to the captain about it and later he told me to go ahead and hammer test. "Aye, aye, sir."

I in turn told the Oil King, BT2 Ronald Donald (yes, that was his name) to do the testing and he in turn delegated the job to the Assistant Oil King, BT3 Phillip Sobrane.

Shortly thereafter, Petty Officer Sobrane came to me, chipping hammer in hand, and said he was going to get started. I said, "Great!" I didn't really think we needed to do a practice session and BSTM didn't really explain how hard the tapping was supposed to be, only the size of the hammer to be used. He had the specified hammer. I told him to carry a notebook with him, and some blue chalk, and mark any bad spots found, if any, both with the chalk and with a notation in his notebook. "Aye aye, sir." I then forgot about the problem and a few days later, Sobrane saw me on deck. "Mr. King, I finished the testing."

"Good, did you find any bad spots?"

"Yes sir, I made eighty-seven holes."

Oh, shit! Who would have dreamed there would be that many? As it turned out some pipes had more than one hole, so it wasn't quite that bad, but it was bad. I notified the shop that some of the fuel oil stub pipes had holes in them. A lead man came by and looked around. He left and a while later two more lead men came on board and looked at the fuel oil stub pipes. Then it was liberty call, but I had the duty.

Almost an hour after liberty call, a full commander from the shipyard came on board and asked to see the CO. When advised the CO was not on board, he demanded to see the chief engineer. "Sorry sir, he is not on board either."

"What is your job"?

"At the moment, sir, I am CDO, but I am also the MPA"

"Did you have anything to do with the damage to the fuel oil stub piping?"

"Well, I ordered the hammer testing, sir." At that he flew into a mad rage. By the time he was done ranting and raving, he had made it clear that I was going to be court-martialed and the charge was going to be sabotage. Then he stormed down the brow.

The next day, I told the new chief engineer about the commander's tirade. He was upset, but coy. He suddenly didn't remember that he had authorized the hammer testing. I suspected the new captain wouldn't remember it either. Later that day, I was shown a message from the shipyard to COMCRUDESPAC in San Diego requesting the latter to convene a general court martial with me as the defendant on a charge of sabotage. It became clear. I was a reservist, my tour was about over and I was going to be hung out to dry so two careerists would be protected.

That night I couldn't sleep. Many thoughts ran through my mind including that this would not be happening to me if former Captain Ely Kirk and former Chief Engineer Al Sherman were still on board. We would be working on a joint defense together rather than plotting to "stick it to the reservist." Then I had another idea. During the course of the overhaul, I had had some dealings with a high-ranking civilian in the shipyard named Harry Grady. He seemed like an honest, levelheaded man and although I didn't know his GS number (civilian pay grade), I suspected he reported directly to the vice commander of the shipyard. Maybe I should go to see him.

By morning I had made up my mind. I grabbed the appropriate volume of BSTM and headed for Mr. Grady's office in the shipyard. I asked his secretary if I could see Mr. Grady, giving her my rank, name and ship. The secretary disappeared and a moment later Mr. Grady came out and escorted me into his large office. I told him I was about to be court-martialed. He said he knew all about it. I asked if he wanted to listen to my side of the story and he said yes, go ahead.

I told Mr. Grady I had personally watched the approval of my work request at the pre-arrival conference in San Diego by both the shipyard and the type commander. That approval had never been cancelled and it was still on the list of jobs to be done. Then I told him about what had happened on the last cruise when NSFO was spewing all over the back of an on-line boiler. Then I opened up BSTM to the key page and turned it so it faced him and showed him how the "hammer test" was specifically authorized. He read the paragraph and then sat there for a minute. Mr. Grady then asked, "Why didn't you come see me about the problem instead of taking things into your own hands? Have I ever refused to see you in the past?"

I didn't have a good answer except to reply, "No, sir." He leaned back in his chair and reflected.

Finally, he started talking. He admitted that the job had never been cancelled and that it was so late in the overhaul that if work didn't begin in the next couple of days, the *Chevalier's* overhaul schedule would have to be extended. He went on to confess that the yard had a shortage of welders and was also building a nuclear submarine, SSN-665, which was way behind schedule because of the same problem. He then further admitted that the yard had unilaterally decided the submarine launching was more important than the *Chevalier's* fuel oil stub piping and the yard had simply decided to neither cancel my job nor to actually start it. The yard would later claim it was a paper snafu and that it just "fell through the cracks."

Mr. Grady then said, "There are no clean hands in this matter ... I will take care of the court martial. Next time, however, come see me first if you have a problem."

I asked, "What do you mean by take care of?"

"Just forget it. There will be no court martial. I will see to it."

I thanked Mr. Grady but didn't tell him there would also be no next time; I was getting very short as they say on the mess decks. When I got back to the ship, the only person I told was Chief Morton. Let the new chief engineer squirm for a few days. I also noted that shipyard pipefitters were already crawling in and around the main engineering spaces working on the fuel oil stub piping.

So I cheerfully carried on with my various duties. A week or two later I looked at a calendar. I had less than ten working days to wrap things up on the *Chevalier*, process out at Treasure Island, pack up personal effects, load the Edsel and drive cross country to law school in Nashville. I went to see the XO and told him I really was leaving and showed him my shipyard tool credit card with my name on it, the only one the ship had. I said if I am not relieved pronto as tool officer, I will be taking the credit card with me to Nashville and the ship will be up the creek without a paddle. Two days later I was relieved as tool officer.

Since my roommates and I all had cars and shipyard parking was at a premium, when duty schedules permitted, we would car pool in one or at most two cars. I had already started going to Treasure Island, jumping through all the separation hoops, but I was generally dismissed by about 1300 and then returned to the ship to continue working on loose ends and the overhaul.

One Friday the DCA and I commuted together in my car. After liberty call, as we got in my car, the DCA asked, "I need to pick something up at the EM Club, it will only take a minute. Do you mind if we stop on the way out?" When we got to the EM Club, he said, "Why don't you come in with me?" I couldn't figure out why, but said, "Okay."

We went in the front door and he started up a staircase like he knew where he was going. At the landing at the top there were double doors, which were closed. He opened a door and there was a roar of "SURPRISE" from about sixty sailors, all of the snipes on the *Chevalier* less the duty section plus the engineering yeoman. I was overwhelmed. I had been to "farewell and following seas" parties before, but I had never heard of one hosted by enlisted crew members for an officer. I was so overwhelmed I proceeded over the next six hours to get very drunk, as did many others. So drunk, in fact, that upon leaving, before I even left the base, I managed to rip the oil pan off the bottom of my engine by hitting a manhole in a parking lot being prepped for pavement. The repairs the next day set me back a tidy sum, but what the hell.

On my last day at Treasure Island, one of the stops was at the separation disbursing officer's office. As I sat in the chair in his office, he was poring over my records. He asked me where had I been: "You are almost eighty days overdue." I told him about all the overhaul problems, that there was no relief on board yet, the chief engineer took thirty days emergency leave, et cetera. He finally said, "Come back in two hours, I need to do some investigating."

So I left and came back in two hours. This time the disbursing officer started talking. He said there was a reason why the Navy planned to separate me in about my 34th month rather than wait until the last minute. He explained that on the third anniversary of my commissioning, I had been promoted to 0-3 ... "Congratulations, Lieutenant, but you are out of uniform. I have also confirmed that while you were UA from Treasure Island, you reported to the ship daily, stood watches, and carried out all duties assigned. I recommended a court martial, but my boss said to forget it, it is not worth pursuing."

I asked, "Then what's the problem?"

He said, "Well, first, when you became an 0-3 over three, you had over sixty days unused leave on the books and now I have to pay you for that leave at the 0-3 over three rate. Second, I also have to pay you the difference between an 0-2 under three and an 0-3 over three for the last 80 days or so ... here are your checks, sign this receipt here."

I looked at the checks. I had never received so much money at one time in my life.

I made it to Nashville at 0200 on the same day I started class at law school at 0800. About three weeks later, the DCA called and announced that the *Chevalier* had been awarded the "Red E" for the prior fiscal year. I was again overwhelmed.

Later I joined the Naval Reserves, for the money. On one of my first drill weekends, on Saturday, the CO of the reserve center said that I was to be given an award. He wouldn't tell me what it is about. On Sunday morning at quarters, the senior reserve officer, a captain, announced, "Lieutenant King, front and center!" When I got up there, he started to read from some proclamation full of bullshit, hyperbole and exaggerations, but when he finished, it dawned on me that I had just been awarded The Secretary of the Navy's Achievement Medal with Combat V. Later, studying the proclamation carefully, I realized it covered the time period starting when I took over as MPA and ending a week before the change of command ceremony in Australia. Undoubtedly the recommendation was one of the last official acts of the *Chevalier's* 13th commanding officer, Captain G. G. Ely Kirk.

From multiple Courts Martial (Sabotage and Failing to Report to Treasure Island as Ordered) to SECNAV Achievement Medal with Combat V in ninety days; that must be some sort of a record.

Footnotes:

The *USS Guitaro (SSN 665)* was launched at Mare Island on July 27, 1968. On May 16, 1969, still tied to the pier at Mare Island while undergoing final outfitting, she starting taking on water and sank in 35 feet of water in fifteen minutes. I always wondered if the tug of war that summer between the *Chevalier* and the *Guitaro* for shipyard pipefitters had anything to do with it.

In May 1996, the Chief of Naval Operations, Admiral Jeremy Boorda, committed suicide. The press had discovered and was about to report that although he too had been awarded the SECNAV Achievement Medal in the 1960s, the Combat 'V' had not been authorized. But he had worn the 'V' anyway for some thirty years. My medal specifically authorized the Combat V, but if given the choice between the medal or the Hail and Farewell party hosted by the ship's snipes at the Mare Island EM Club, the autographed card that came with it, and the watch they gave me, I would have opted for the party, card and watch without hesitation. It meant a whole lot more to me.

A DEAD SHIP

BY ROBERT TEGROEN

After a hiatus of nine years in the Active Status Pool of the USNR, I joined the Selective Reserve Crew (SELRES) of the *USS Vammen (DE-644)* in 1963. Previously in 1953 I had been a snipe on a turbine reduction gear tin can but now I had to learn how a turbo-electric drive worked. The system was basic and very flexible to the needs of propelling the ship through the water in all kinds of situations. But the ship had been laid down in 1943, commissioned in July 1944 and she had been involved in several South Pacific Island campaigns, suffered propeller damage from an underwater collision of unknown origin, and had been a general work horse for the navy.

Vammen had also participated in the Korean War, and had recently returned from an active duty call-up that had lasted from Oct. 1961 to August 1962 that saw her engaged in naval activities in the Western Pacific including Vietnam. So with a ship and her equipment being as we say in the horse business, "rode hard and put away wet," you just don't run over to Serve Mart or the Buffalo Pump Company for parts; there aren't any for a twenty-plus year old ship living on borrowed time. My first ACDUTRA job in '63 was to repair the laundry machine; it was busted, well, at least the cast iron spur gear was. I welded it up and we had clean skivvies for the cruise.

Then one weekend I was told that we had access to a target ship and might be able to find some parts for *Vammen*. Men from several departments joined us for the *strip ship* operation and we drove out on the Long Beach mole where I saw a forlorn *Fletcher*-class tied up all by herself at one of the piers, heavy towing chains draped from the bullnose indicating this lady was not going anywhere under her own power. I did not note her name, I cannot recall even if she had her number visible; I just recall that she was a Greyhound, a

Tin Can, a Destroyer, my favorite ship; but I doubted I would find anything for *Vammen's* different engineering plant.

Our group was met by the caretaker who told us that we could take anything from the interior, but nothing could be removed from the exterior. I assumed that had to do with a radar signature. He also warned us that navigating through the interior could be hazardous because there were holes and there was no power or lights. I ducked in the first midships watertight door and Damn Sam, almost fell into the after fireroom because a big hole had been cut in the passageway so a fuel oil pump could be removed. There was black oil smeared all over the deck and bulkhead along with the pungent smell of the NSFO. I chose another direction and explored more, noting the absence of something from this — no, not the parts, not the pump, there was something else that was gone from this ship: I think it was life.

There were no lights, not even the comforting red glow of the red emergency lights I remember when I came back to my ships after a liberty on the beach. There was no familiar soft hum of the ventilation blowers anywhere, not even from the enginerooms that always seemed to beckon for me to visit; what's on line? Who's on watch? Maybe a snipe just sitting alone in front of the throttle board by himself reading a Louie L'Amour novel. I had been there, done that. No, all the engineering spaces were just deep, dark, empty holes devoid of life now; I had no desire to descend into that. I thought of the mess deck where there was always somebody reading or a game of acey-deucey in progress, but no, not enough light to venture there, or even to the Goat Locker where I thought I might find a chief passing the time. There was no one from the past to find, really.

I kept searching for some signature of previous life, occasionally finding some of our team removing some part — a motor generator for the radio, bunk racks, whatever; but still I found not one thing that would give me a clue about the memories of the people that make up the life of a ship. Reaching the bridge I noticed the brass speaking tubes that connected the bridge with CIC and using a hacksaw, cut out enough so I could later make a speaking tube on the *Vammen's* Main Control upper level to the lower level.

Then I ventured into Officer's Country and looking into the long empty drawers, found a scrap of paper with the scrawled message, "FN Jones, 456446789, reported aboard 10/10/53." Now I had at least a small connection with this ship's life; there had been real tin can sailors who made her move, made her communicate, had made the ventilation blowers hum, given light and life to this now lonely hulk. I wish I had kept that scrap of paper.

Footnote: The fate of that *Fletcher* tin can was probably the bottom of the ocean, I don't know. I do know *Vammen* went to the bottom on 18 February 1971 after being used as a target.

TIME AND TIDE

BY JACK DINEEN

The US Navy's East Coast operating areas off the Virginia Capes through Florida can be most unforgiving for the ships and crews that learn their deadly trades and hone their fighting skills prior to each major deployment. During the Cold War it was not unusual to have war games several times each year for Carrier Battle Groups to effectively train as a group. Usually, this entailed two CVBGs and NATO ships from many nations since the primary object was to train to fight our way to Europe in the event that the Soviet Union had attacked Western Europe through the Fulda Gap in Germany.

While one CVBG played the part of the Soviets, the other took on the role of the US Navy and allied NATO naval forces. A typical Carrier Battle Group in these years consisted of a carrier, several cruisers (guided missile equipped), several guided missile destroyers (Terrier and Tarter Missiles), one or two older all-gun destroyers, one of the newest *Spruance*-class anti-submarine warfare destroyers, several frigates, one of which that carried guided missiles, replenishment ships for fuel, food and munitions and lastly several nuclear powered submarines. It was a large capable grouping of ships designed to protect the carrier and her strike aircraft.

During late January and early February, 1980, while serving as an Operations Specialist Third Class aboard the *USS King (DDG-41)*, a *Farragut*-class DDG, I had the responsibility of acting as the understudy for the eventual promotion to Combat Information Center (CIC) Watch Supervisor. We normally worked a strenuous at-sea schedule of five hours on watch followed by seven hours off and then seven hours on and five hours off, a *port and starboard* watch schedule. Most off-duty time was filled with general quarters drills, man overboard drills, underway replenishments, anti-surface, anti-air and anti-submarine warfare exercises, personnel qualifications for advancement and studying for the coveted Enlisted Surface Warfare Pin (ESWS), attempting to eat, and the very popular and time-consuming "clean the ship" routine the XO loved.

Operation Safe-Passage was a vital part of learning the art of war at sea. It lasted the better part of three weeks. At the end we would then be certified to deploy to South America for six months the following May for a UNITAS cruise. This NATO training exercise, code named Operation Safe-Passage 80 began with us leaving our homeport of Norfolk Virginia, home to the US Navy's Second Fleet, and transiting to the southern operation areas off the Coast of Florida and the northernmost regions of the Caribbean Sea. This was a welcomed exercise, for we left behind the very cold days and bitter cold nights of the winter of 1980. Midway through the operation we visited Mayport, Florida where much-needed liberty was anticipated and we had the opportunity to also enjoy liberty with NATO sailors, primarily from Canada and the United Kingdom.

Prior to leaving Mayport Naval Station, the weather was nasty, even for northern Florida, where Mayport is located. Our departure was uneventful and soon the battle group was in formation as we steamed north to the second part of the operation, north to perhaps some of the worst at-sea weather and conditions any mariner could experience in the Northern Hemisphere, the often violent waters off of Cape Hatteras, North Carolina.

What I witnessed shortly thereafter, while on the *King's* bridge was something out of a movie.

First, the *King* was 512 feet long with a 52 foot beam and a 26 foot draft that had her looking sleek and slender. She was also quite top-heavy and in heavy seas she rolled like a drunken sailor. *King* at times would approach 50 degree rolls to both port and starboard as well as plowing her bow into large waves, quite literally keeping the crew up all night and day. In front of *King*, at a range of several thousand yards, was a Canadian corvette with twin propellers. She was a small ship compared to *King* and as we entered very heavy seas off of the coasts of the Carolinas this ship violently pitched forward, dug her bow into the seas and her screws came out of the water for all to see. It was the first and only time I ever witnessed that in my four-plus years on active duty, three years and eight months of which were aboard *King*.

We exercised through each day and night learning our specialties and all that was nautical in a Carrier Battle Group, including life guard during carrier flight operations, where we were stationed 1000 yards behind the carrier to retrieve any downed aviators who had to eject from their planes while attempting to land on the pitching and rolling American sovereign territory. We also practiced underway replenishments to take on fuel from the carrier and other replenishment ships. We also had the chance to fire our weapons systems, which included the Terrier SM-2 anti-air warfare missile and the single 5-inch, 54-caliber Mount 51 gun in both anti-air and anti-surface modes. *King* additionally carried the Mk 46 torpedo and the standard ASROC anti-submarine rocket system. Onward went the exercises, testing men, tactics and all ships systems. It was a physically demanding environment being surrounded by dangerous weather, seas and modern at-sea combat training.

The night of February 6th was the most violent a night at sea that I ever endured or cared to experience. The captain had placed all weather decks off limits due to *King's* low freeboard and the proximity of her main decks to the raging sea. His night orders directed that this message be relayed via the ship's internal communication system or the 1MC for all crew to know and obey. All relieving watch standers on the bridge and CIC were to verify the night orders to ensure the ship and crew's safety. This was standard operational procedure aboard *King*.

Throughout the night and early hours of February 7th *King* rolled and violently pitched throughout the night. I ended my watch at 2400 hours after relieving the previous watch at 1500 hours. It was a tough watch with the seas being so violent. We rolled towards 50 degrees numerous times and maneuvered to find the less violent wave actions, to not be locked in irons, to spare *King* from as much damage topside as possible. The commander of the battle group gave all commanding officers the leeway to maneuver their ships to lessen the dangers to ships and crews. No one really had much sleep that night because of the storm, a classic nor'easter, which roared up from the Gulf of Mexico and along the Eastern seaboard of the United States.

The following morning the seas had seemed to abate somewhat, but the wind was still strong. Reveille was sounded at 0600 hours and breakfast was served shortly thereafter. I had breakfast with my CIC watchstanders, our first real meal in almost 48 hours, due to the cooks not being able to cook in the violent storm we were caught in. I remember not hearing the message to stand clear of the weather decks due to the wave action.

King's crew mess decks were almost amidships and over the main engineering compartment where her propulsion watch was maintained. Just aft of the mess decks there were passageways that led out to a water tight door which led to the ship's main deck, amidships. My fellow CIC watchstanders and I went towards this water tight door, on the starboard side, and peered out to a much calmer sea than that of the past few days. We exited the ship on to the starboard side main deck. *King* was rolling some, but in calm waters she rolled, too. I took the opportunity to walk some 100 feet to the first ladder leading to the O-2 level or the first deck above *King's* main deck. It was an uneventful walk along with my CIC crew. We then climbed to the second deck, O-2 level, entered the ship's skin and climbed the inner ladder ways to the bridge and CIC to relieve the midnight watch.

We relieved the watch and were updated on the status of the battle group as well as *King's* condition after several days of serious pounding by the violent seas. The *USS Radford (DD-968)*, a new *Spruance*-class ASW destroyer, had suffered serious damage to her sonar dome, when her bow had completely risen out of the water and then slammed back into the sea. The *USS Nimitz (CVN-68)*, a nuclear aircraft carrier, reported damage to her forward sponsons from a huge wave that broke over her bow and rolled down her flight deck. Several other ships reported damage to their main decks and equipment located on these decks. *King* had serious damage aft along the main deck where the aluminum superstructure pulled apart from her steel hull. There was a fire in the ship's emergency power battery room after a huge wave slammed her aft along the port side which broke off a watertight door, allowing salt sea water to contact the batteries. This fire was quickly put out. Numerous firefighting station hoses topside were washed away, along with sections of the lifelines. It was a hard night topside on *King*.

Shortly before 0800, Muster on Station was called over the 1MC. All hands were accounted for and the Executive Officer ordered the night's topside damage repaired since the seas were somewhat calmer that morning. Boatswain's Mates and Hull Technicians turned to, to fix what they could and to re-rig missing lifelines. Just around this time I relieved the watch on the bridge as the JA talker between the bridge and CIC.

Abruptly, a huge rogue wave appeared from nowhere and slammed into the starboard side of *King* and immediately the aft lookout stationed above the missile house (to remain above the fierce seas) reported, "Man overboard!" Immediately I relayed this information to CIC so they could begin the man overboard Dead Reckoning Tracer (DRT) plot to commence Search and Rescue (SAR) operations. The officer of the deck immediately ordered a Williamson turn to clear the screws from those washed overboard. The captain entered the bridge and assumed the deck and the conn. Immediate flash radio message traffic was sent to all in the battle group. Air assets from the carrier and land assets were launched. It was too rough to launch the motor whaleboat.

The Atlantic off of Cape Hatteras during February is cold, at about 40 degrees and with the wind it made it much colder. Your expectation of surviving a fall overboard in this weather was measured in the tens of minutes if not sooner, and those who were washed overboard were not wearing any protective clothing other than dungarees and foul weather jackets. Soon a muster was taken and it was determined that four Kingsmen were missing with several others seriously injured, with open wounds to the legs, cut to the bone, after being crushed against the ship by this rogue wave. They were being treated in sickbay which is about where the wave had struck along the starboard side. They would have to wait to be evacuated via helicopter.

I was relieved on the bridge as JA talker and assumed the duties as the operator of the DRT to keep the track on the ship and where we believed the men overboard were in the water and to coordinate the SAR operations with the watch supervisor. *King* came around and positioned itself so that the ship would block the wind from the four men in the sea, essentially to have the ship come to the men and not have the wind blow them away.

Two were spotted in the water, Petty Officer McGuiness; ironically the ship's rescue swimmer, and one other, Petty Officer Bilicek. Petty Officer McGuiness and Petty Officer Bilicek were close together, with Seamen Traylor and Campbell being unaccounted for and unseen. Bilicek was beginning to succumb to the cold of the water, tired from swimming and treading water, and he decided to take off his foul weather jacket. As *King* maneuvered to pick them up, Bilicek went under just several minutes after going over the side. He was never seen again and shortly thereafter McGuiness was hauled aboard using ropes. Seamen Traylor and Campbell were not seen again.

Several of the battle group's ships assisted in the search for the missing *King* sailors. Aviation assets from the carrier and the *Radford* also searched for them. Land-based planes and helicopters arrived, but in a fashion that was too late due to the water temperature. After Petty Officer McGuiness was aboard he was looked over by the ship's independent-duty corpsman and was found to be suffering from the effects of the frigid waters. He relayed that the wave came out of nowhere and was towering, smashing them against the ship's skin on the main deck. He believed that at least one of the missing was most likely dead from the trauma of the wave crushing him against a ship's fender. He could not provide information on the fourth sailor.

We searched for hours hoping to retrieve the two missing crew members. A MedEvac SH-3 arrived to take off the two most seriously injured. Flight quarters in the now-confused sea state was a dangerous operation, but we got it done and our injured were en route to Portsmouth Naval Hospital, the closest Navy hospital. As dusk approached, SAR operations were suspended, with all hope of retrieving the missing now long gone. *King* was then ordered to return to Norfolk with the wounded *Radford*. The following morning we arrived in Norfolk to see to our injured and remember our dead. The damage could wait for another day.

Death came to those in the sea from the cold, enveloping their faces when first contact with the water was made. It began in their legs, traveled to their waists, then to their chests and they began to fade until they slipped beneath the surface of the ocean. Their Earthly resting place known only to God and on Judgment Day, the Sea Shall Give Up Her Dead in the Certain Knowledge that their duty is done. Fine men these three were. Sailors, shipmates and friends all.

Time has faded some of my memories of that morning twenty-seven years ago and the tides of the oceans have changed the waves in uncountable ways. I still recall the above like it was yesterday and I can see the faces of those young men who were lost forever. I hope that time and tides have brought peace to their families, for they will never be forgotten by their shipmates. RIP Petty Officer Bilicek, Seaman Campbell and Seaman Traylor.

"YOU'VE GOT MAIL"

BY ROBIN SMITH

I have a CNN feed in my office, and can keep up with daily events while I work. Late in the summer of '03 I was able to watch a carrier return to Pier 11 at the Norfolk Naval Base from a record deployment in the Persian Gulf.

The CNN camera crew showed hundreds of family members crowding the pier waiting for their sailors to come ashore. My chest puffed up with pride in our sailors for the mission they had just completed, and my eyes misted up at the sight of so many cheering and sobbing relatives lining the pier. My mind was carried back to a time nearly thirty years earlier when I was a young sailor aboard the *USS Spruance (DD-963)* returning home after a lengthy time at sea. I never had family waiting for me on the pier, but I could share in the excitement of my shipmates as they scanned the crowd expectantly for their loved ones. Then I would watch them charge ashore into the arms of a loving wife, or girlfriend. It was very moving. A destroyer doesn't attract a very large crowd compared to that gathered for over 5,000 men and women serving aboard the carrier.

The camera showed wives with tears streaming down their faces. Some of them were veterans of navy deployments, and had their teenage children with them. Others were very young, and held babies that were born while their daddies were at sea. These young brides seemed no more than babies themselves. Regardless of their ages, being a single mom is hard work. Golf-widows have nothing on Navy or Marine wives.

There were dads, and moms, too, and they were also filled with excitement watching the carrier maneuver through the Hampton Roads Bridge/Tunnel on its way to pier 11. Watching all of this just brought all my old feelings and memories back to the surface.

Slowly the haze-gray behemoth was wrestled alongside the pier by several tugboats. Lines came ashore, then came the announcement, "Moored! Shift colors." The ship was now officially home, and her deployment ended. It was now a matter of putting the brow in place, and the liberty sections to come ashore.

The reporter was working the crowd asking the expected questions while everyone continued to wait. He stopped to ask a proud father what he was thinking. One of the questions he asked was, "When was the last time you heard from your son?"

"Oh, we were in touch daily through e-mail."

What?? The emotional steamroller I was driving came to an abrupt stop! All of my emotions now turned to disbelief at that simple statement. It shouldn't have surprised me as much as it did. After all, e-mail is a very big part of modern life these days. Still, the poignancy of the moment had evaporated.

In the days of Lord Nelson sailors were completely cut off from any family they might have had when they set sail. Mail would have been nice, but the logistics of the time made it impossible to deliver letters to ships at sea. It was not a big problem since the typical enlisted man could neither read, nor write. That was a skill possessed by the officer corps which was made up of men from the upper classes. Over time the literacy rate among sailors improved, and so did the supply lines. By World War Two logistics made it possible to ship letters and care packages to sailors and marines on the front lines. Still, a letter may have been in the pipeline for a long time before reaching the addressee.

By the mid-1970s, when I was a young sailor, the time mail spent in transit had been greatly reduced, but it may still have been a couple of weeks before a letter from home arrived aboard a ship, and a few more weeks would pass before a reply would show up in someone's mailbox. Separation was still a problem for Navy and Marine families.

Crew fatigue set in in a matter of days during a cruise, and routine further dulled the senses. The daily routine at sea had sailors working, eating, or sleeping. During lunchtime bodies of sailors were strewn about the topside decks sunning themselves as they caught a "nooner" before "turning-to" again. In the evenings a spirited game of euchre could be found here and there, and some stalwarts even found the energy to watch movies in the evening. In general, though, the crewmen of a navy ship were whipped after a week at sea.

This all changed when word got out that the ship was scheduled for underway replenishment. Ships at sea periodically pull alongside a supply vessel, or aircraft carrier, to re-supply, and with any luck a bag of mail would be included with the goods. As soon as the word starting making the rounds that mail was on board, sailors whose butts were dragging suddenly were re-energized. The air aboard ship was electric, and time passed slowly. Finally, the boatswain's mate of the watch announces "Mail call!" and mail petty officers all over the ship explode into action.

A dozen men converge on the mailroom. On the *Spruance* this was nothing more than a closet-sized space with a barred window. Our postal clerk sat on a stool behind the bars, looking like a jailed gnome. "Hey PC, they going to allow you a conjugal visit soon?" someone would quip. This would be followed by nervous laughter from excited sailors. "Here's your mail, funny guy, git outta here!" came the reply.

The mail petty officers would return to their division spaces to hand out the mail. In my case that meant the chartroom. Having only five or six guys in the navigation division meant mail was handed out quickly, and we could each get down to the business of reading.

Guys who got mail walked on clouds for days, letters peeking out from pockets. After several days the sheets of paper became thin as toilet paper from frequent handling. Each man would find his own quiet spot somewhere onboard ship. They would then pull out their letters and savor each written word. Some letters were doused in "foo-foo juice" and filled the air with an aura of romance. Sailors fortunate enough to receive such letters normally had smiles on their faces that went from ear to ear. It wasn't unusual to see these guys with the pages of their letter pressed up to their noses. "Careful Smitty, you'll inhale those letters!" A shit-eating grin, a friendly signal to move on, and the sailor was lost in his sweetheart's letter again.

Others weren't as lucky, and would have to wait for the next mail call for notes from home. Mail petty officers had to watch these guys and warn of any indication of emotional problems that might arise. These cases were far and few between. However, sometimes a letter did come that could be more devastating than not getting any mail at all.

"Dear John, oh how I hate to write …" Every military man with a sweetheart back home dreaded the Dear John letter. Mine came while I was at sea off the Virginia Capes OpArea. The mail had been brought aboard following an unrep with the *USS America (CVA-66)*. I searched my parcel of mail, separating my own from the others. My fiancée's letter went into my breast pocket to be read when I was done handing out the rest of the mail. I then returned to the berthing compartment and found myself alone. I was excited, and sat down at a table pulling the letter out of my pocket and carefully opening it. As I read the smile I wore slowly faded, and my spirit sank. Dear Johns are not expected, and they have the emotional impact of a sucker punch. Had I been standing, I would have dropped to the deck just like 200-lbs of potatoes. I slumped in my chair and sat in stunned silence, maintaining my composure as best I could.

What could I have done to save my relationship with my then wife-to-be? I couldn't just take up a collection of quarters from my shipmates and run out to a pay phone on the pier to call my darling. The nearest payphone was hundreds of miles away. I had plenty of time to write a letter, since it would have been days before mail went out again. At best it would have been a month from the day my sweetie launched her missile that a response would have arrived. I figured there would be little point in it by then. I let her go.

As each veteran will tell you, the young sailors of today have it easier. They have many comforts that we older sailors didn't have in our day. Of course, this is a good thing, although enduring the hardships seems to make us saltier. E-mail has made life easier for the lovesick sailor. Sailors can now watch their children grow up in near-real time by downloading photos. Likewise, the sailor's travels can be shared with their family just as easily. E-mail also means the modern Navy wife has lost some autonomy in family matters, since e-mail now allows a husband at sea to communicate in near-real time. Dear Johns will never go away, but they may not happen as often. Had e-mail been available to me I could have saved my relationship, and it may have prevented my getting a Dear John in the first place. I would be married to a different woman, and have a different set of children. Life can be that precarious!

The announcement, "Mail Call!" is slowly being replaced by the now familiar, "You've got mail!" The postal clerk is discovering his mailbag is getting lighter and lighter all the time. I don't expect the job to disappear entirely (no one has figured out how to download cookies yet), but it may become a subspecialty of other Navy administrative ratings. If it makes life at sea easier for those who go in harm's way, I'm all for it.

THE NEW NAVY UNDERWAY

BY JIM KELLY

From the age of sail I am reminded of a sentence penned by a well known sailor, clearly a man of vision: "The sea will grant each man new hope, as sleep brings dreams of home." — *Christopher Columbus*

Who among us having felt the movement of a ship beneath our feet, and having spent time at sea, long for the return of these simple pleasures? On February 7, 2001 I found myself standing on the 01 level, aft, with my friend and shipmate, Roger "Bud" Lincoln (IC2) whose great-great-grandfather captained and built ships sailing forth from Bath and Damariscotta, Maine. Beside us stood JOC Richard Gorham, USNR, our Media Escort, and long time friend of Bud Lincoln. As it turns out, Dick also has sea captains in his lineage dating back to the 1790's, with ships out of Searsport, Maine. Together we watched lines being cast off fore and aft as *USS Winston S. Churchill (DDG-81)*, the newest *Aegis* guided-missile destroyer in the US Navy, prepared to get underway.

This evolution has been accomplished thousands of times over the years. The phrase "Bath-built ships" has been a hallmark for many of those years. The scene at Bath Iron Works on this morning was routine enough for those who carry out the day-to-day business of shipbuilding. Even so, this was a special day as the men and women who had built the new *Arleigh Burke*-class destroyer put down their tools, finished phone calls, stepped away from their work, and watched with admiration and pride as the colors were shifted and this ship began to move. Aboard ship the idle chatter of sailors and guests of the Navy trailed away, a quiet descended upon the yard as all eyes were riveted to the sight of this powerful ship being pulled by two tugs out into the current of the Kennebec River. I was touched by this sentiment from the people at BIW, which came down to us loud and clear from all corners of the yard. It was palpable and it was genuine. The impact of going to sea again and being witness to these events did transcend the years that separate mariners from ships and the sea. As I silently pondered this, a chill went through me. I have since asked myself, was this the result of the cold, crisp, clear Maine air coming across the deck that morning? I think not.

Upon being cast off by our tugs the ship immediately surged under power against the current. Her twin variable-pitch propellers powered by four General Electric LM-2500 gas turbines thrust our 9,600 tons out into mid-stream. The route to the sea here in Maine is a tortured route, fraught with hazards. Careless shiphandling could bring disaster. With typical British humor, Lt. Angus N. P. Essenhigh, RN, the ship's Navigator and the first in a line of succession of Royal Navy liaison officers assigned to this ship, was quoted later by Jack Dorsey of the *Virginian-Pilot*, "I believe it to be cruel and unusual punishment for navigators to have to do that for the first time." Lt. Essenhigh and the navigation team brought the new ship through the hazards without a hitch, despite having no more than two feet of water beneath her keel at times.

BIW had hired a helicopter and photographer to catch the sight on film for posterity as their ship made for open water. Later, at sea, the ship attained full power with a rooster tail of 25 feet or more while making 34.5 knots.

It appears likely that this sort of fanfare will follow this ship for quite some time. The name Winston S. Churchill evokes memories and stirs emotions in our country but especially so across the foam, in England. This British connection will be highly publicized in the worlds' press as she makes her first transatlantic crossing in August. Port visits in Great Britain are scheduled at Greenwich, Plymouth, and the large Royal Navy base at Portsmouth. Operations with Her Majesty's forces and those of Norway are planned.

For those who have not gotten a close-up view of this class of ship, let me try to put this into perspective for you. Basically, what we have is an all-steel construction destroyer approaching and even exceeding cruiser dimensions! As an example, the *Omaha*-class light cruiser measured 555 feet, DDG-81 comes in at 513 feet. The *Churchill* is actually wider in beam by several feet, also very much deeper in draft and well over 2,000 tons heavier in displacement than the *Omaha*-class. In comparison with WWI and WWII destroyers, the *Arleigh Burke*-class would weigh in with twice the beam and many times over in tonnage. Any attempt to compare firepower would be difficult, if not downright impossible. For openers, this ship is the first in the fleet to mount the new Mk 45 5-inch, 62-caliber gun which fires a 120-pound ERGM (Extended Range Guided Munition) projectile, out to a maximum range of 63 miles — with uncanny accuracy! Then there is the CIWS (Close-In Weapons System), a Gatling Gun called the Phalanx, Mk 15 Mod 12, which spits out 20mm rounds at the astonishing rate of 3,000 rounds per minute. DDG-81 carries one forward and aft. When you add the LAMPS (Light Airborne Multi-Purpose System) helicopter and her vertical-launch guided missiles with a mix of missile types, you come away with an unprecedented lethality.

The *Winston S. Churchill* is well suited to the 21st century with her stealth configuration. All rails and stanchions on her weather decks are angled, and this continues with all bulkheads and superstructure. Radar cannot get a firm return with so many glancing hits. I believe Sir Winston Churchill, whose name she bears, and who had an eye for a good ship, would surely revel in the rake of her mast, her overall design, construction and fire power.

Chief Gorham, Bud and I disembarked upon arrival at Portsmouth, New Hampshire. The next day the ship got underway for points south. New York City was to be the first stop and then on to Norfolk, Virginia. The experiences over a 24-hour period were enlightening and will become a lasting memory for us. It has been mentioned that 40% of the crew had never been to sea. They were eager to leave the confines of the builder's yards and go to sea. In fairness to this segment of the crew and to the Navy, I can remember when I had never gone to sea before, as may be the case with many reading this account. We all served our country, learned quickly and survived the experience, and in doing so, became the better for it. As Chief Gorham says, "*Churchill* is a technological marvel, but the true heart and soul of the new ship is her crew, made up of young energetic sailors, and seasoned chiefs with a group of hard-charging officers led by a dynamic commanding officer, CDR Michael T. Franken, USN. The *Churchill* will do well. This crew is the embodiment of the next generation of sailors; highly skilled, technologically literate, excited to be at sea. I like this crew and I know they will do us proud."

"In war; Resolution ~ In Peace; Goodwill."

DON'T GET PISSED. RE-ENLIST!

BY LARRY PALLOZOLA

It was a late summer morning in 1976. I fell in to what was supposed to pass for ranks with the rest of the motley crew of Second Division. The sun was at my back, and it would soon dry off the condensation on the 01-level torpedo deck. Off to my right I could hear the traffic on the Magnolia Bridge. Over my shoulder to the left I could see Seattle's famed Space Needle and further into the distance, Mount Rainier stood majestic and proud. I would have liked to just soak in the sights and sounds of this fine morning, but that was not to be. This was my first time at quarters with my new division. Grabassin' and pissin' n moanin' were in full swing. Joel Herr, whom I met earlier in the berthing compartment, was bitching about something or other. Facing us was a bearded, sawed off, stocky figure of a man. He shifted his weight impatiently from left foot to right. His short sleeve and stenciling told me this was PO1 Haggerty. When Joel Herr had completed his diatribe, PO1 Haggerty said to him, "Hey. Don't get pissed. Re-enlist!"

To this day, I have no idea what the hell he meant by that. His statement and so many other absurdities wove their way into the fabric of what became my *McKean* experience. And now, nearly thirty years later, I am dredging up these long-forgotten memories. Don't get pissed. Re-enlist. I can't help chuckling as I remember it. I take my eyes off the road for a second and see that my wife has nodded off. Let her sleep. Traffic is light on Oregon Highway 20, and the rain has let up some. In about an hour I'll fill the tank and get some coffee. I should make Seattle by 3 a.m. Plenty of time to remember the *McKean*.

Plenty of revived memories, too. Returning from our vacation, driving through redwood country and along the Pacific coast on US Route 101, we found ourselves coming up on Newport, Oregon, a city the *McKean* visited, sometime back around 1980. For some reason, I felt compelled to pull off the road and search out the waterfront area of that long-ago liberty stop. I searched both sides of the river before I found some familiar sights.

The working waterfront of Newport is still a working waterfront, primarily focused on commercial fishing and crabbing. However, I notice, the chamber of commerce has dubbed it Newport's "Historic Waterfront" area. I pull over and park on Bay Street. The sun has set, and the whole area seems eerily deserted. I get out and look across at a ship tied up at the pier across the way. It looks to be some sort of intercoastal freighter. Painted on her hull, roughly amidships, I can make out the words HISTORIC VESSEL. She must be some sort of museum ship, but the words, historic vessel, add a touch of irony to the scene, as this is exactly where the *USS McKean* tied up so many years ago.

Before liberty call was passed, the crew was told to wear the "new" crackerjack uniform. "It will be a big hit with the local folks," we were told. I did as advised. Out on the street, I noticed that I would have to walk a bit to get my land legs back. I liked to walk, so I began to wander about the waterfront, exploring, until my ill-fitting dress shoes told me it was time to turn back. It was more than just my shoes that made me uncomfortable, though. Walking through the local populace in uniform reminded me that the general never-been-in-the-service civilians still hadn't gotten over our misunderstood involvement in Vietnam. They still looked down on the military as baby killers. No words were exchanged, but I could just tell that we didn't belong in their town. I didn't feel welcome in their town.

On my way back, I noticed some shipmates going into a local bar. Maybe I'll feel welcome amongst my own crew, I thought. I went in and found most of the *McKean* crew hanging out there. One of the snipes called me over from the back of the room. He sat at a table with a few more snipes. "Go get a beer," he said. Chalk up one more absurdity. Generally, the snipes had an attitude against Second Division, but for some reason tonight I was welcome.

That bar, as I remember, wasn't even a block from where we had tied up. I turn my back to the historic vessel, and start walking. Sure enough, there it is. The Barge Inn, only now it's The *Historic* Barge Inn. It looks like they added another pool table, but otherwise not much has changed. As I remember, throughout much of our liberty there, most *McKean* sailors never went beyond the Barge Inn. Above the door is a sign proclaiming the Historic Barge Inn to be "Home of the Winos, Dingbats, & Riff-Raff." That, too, hasn't changed. I step back from the door. Fear not, old friend, I'm not a ghost come to haunt you. I'm just an old sailor, passing through.

When I left the Barge Inn that night in 1980, I went back to the ship. The next day, liberty call went down at noon. Instead of crackerjacks, I wore my civvies: a flannel shirt and jeans, motorcycle jacket, watch cap, and a comfortable pair of boots. I felt much more at ease as I blended in, anonymously, with the good people of Newport. I went for a long walk. Let's see … I passed the Barge Inn, and … Yes, this looks like it. I turned this corner, and walked up this long steep hill through a residential area, and …

I go back to the car. It's raining, and quite dark out, but if I'm right, at the top of the hill I'll come up on a major road. Right on the corner was where I found that sporting goods store. And, sure enough, it's still there. That's where I bought the big crab pot. I brought it back to the ship, tied on some chicken bones for bait, and dropped it off the fantail. In no time at all, I had ten big Dungeness crabs. What did I do with them? They were live and feisty, so I took them to one of the cooks. For a cut, one crab, he cooked them all for me, and even wrapped them in aluminum foil. Then, I needed to find a place to keep them until we got back to Seattle. I went to the goat locker. For a cut, two crabs this time, they allowed me to keep them in their freezer. Such a deal! I tell this story to my wife. She loves steamed crab, so I figure she'll get a laugh out of my story. She does. Turning the car around, I head back down the hill. The rain is light but steady. Back at Bay Street, I try to remember what else happened.

After securing my stash of Dungeness crabs, I went for a walk up Bay Street. I passed the Barge Inn, looking for a decent place for supper. That's how I came across Mo's. It was a small place, full of local folks. They were all quite friendly, and I was quickly pulled into their conversation. They asked me what I did, assuming I worked on one of the fishing boats across the street. I was almost hesitant to tell them the truth, afraid to break the spell, but I told them I came in on the *McKean*, the destroyer tied up a few piers down. They said that by the way I was dressed, they assumed I was one of the local folks, but, "Hey, you're alright. Have a beer."

I turn right onto Bay street. There it is, not even two blocks up. I park the car in front, and we go in. The place is just as small as I remember it, and I'm pleased to find that the folks are just as friendly. We order a couple of local microbrews and some mighty tasty chowder. On the wall I see behind glass some very yellowed news clippings and photos about when Robert F Kennedy visited Mo's. I remember those from years ago. And, the garage door in the front wall is still there. Some things are different, though. For one thing, they weren't selling Mo's T-shirts and ballcaps. Another thing they had back then were the big outdoor-style tables with bench seats. And that uproots another memory.

The next day, I was just hanging around on the ship when no-longer-PO1, but now-Chief Haggerty came by. I had become a bit wary of him ever since he got religion. It was bad enough when he became a born-again Christian, but then for some reason he got a wild hair up his ass and became Mormon. Now, there are few situations more difficult to be tactful around than when somebody in authority tries to convert you. I mean, whenever FN Harold "of Truth" Scott came around thumping on his bible, proclaiming, "I used to be burned out on acid, but now I'm burned out on the Lord," it was easy to tell him to take a flying fuck at the moon. But that's not so easy with the chief of your own division. So anyway, Chief Haggerty came by wanting to chat. Not about work, and not about my evil ways, but just to talk, like buddies, or something. It was weird. So, ironically, I did the Christian thing. I judged not, lest (something or other), and gave him the benefit of the doubt. I suspect he must have thumped the bible once too often in the goat locker, and got threatened with a good thumping in retaliation if he didn't shut the fuck up and get out. Anyway, I said, "Hey, let's do lunch." I took him to Mo's. We sat at one of those picnic tables, and when some touristy-looking folks came in, and there were no tables available, I suggested they have a seat at ours. There was plenty of room. Besides, I figured that if some strangers were nice enough to be hospitable and friendly to an out-of-town dude like me, then I should probably do the same for somebody else.

On I-5 now. The rain has all but stopped, as I pull in to a truck stop. My Dodge is sucking fumes, and I could sure use that coffee right about now. So, what else can I remember about those days? On the way out of Newport Bay, I seem to remember that time and tide were critical concerns, as far as clearing the bridge without scraping the bottom. All in all, it was a pretty enjoyable liberty stop.

I stayed with the *McKean* until her decommissioning. I had some very good times, and to be honest, not that many bad times. However, there sure was an awful lot that never made much sense. Ah, but then ... Hell. Don't get pissed. Re-enlist.

SCURVY DOGS, GREEN WATER AND GUNSMOKE

FIFTY YEARS IN

US NAVY DESTROYERS

"This is how I remember my time in the Fleet - stories, people, incidents. A navy has ships, but men bring those ships to life. Service in the Navy is exciting, hard, funny, boring, and many other things best told by the men who were there. Give this book to someone who may join the Navy, and they'll get a better picture of shipboard life than from any recruiter. Give this to someone who's been in the Navy, his eyes will get misty, and then he'll start telling his own stories. And of course, these stories are all absolutely true." — **Larry Bond**, author of *Red Phoenix, Dangerous Ground* and *The Mighty Fallen*

"Deck apes, snipes, and powder monkeys alike will just eat up these evocative and entertaining tales of life in the United States destroyer fleet. Smartly told, irreverent and fun, *Scurvy Dogs, Green Water and Gunsmoke* upholds the honor of the surface navy and captures the big-hearted spirit of the tin can sailor of every generation. This book belongs on every Navy man's shelf." — **James D. Hornfischer**, author of *Ship of Ghosts* and *The Last Stand of the Tin Can Sailors*

Printed in the United States
203134BV00004B/67-93/P